How Could This
HAPPEN?

Finding Your Way ...

When Tragedy Strikes

Kristi Fowler, LMFT

HOW COULD THIS HAPPEN?

Finding Your Way When Tragedy Strikes

Every effort has been made to obtain acknowledgements for the quoted material in this book. If any required acknowledgements have been omitted, or any rights overlooked, it is unintentional. Please notify the publisher of any omission and it will be rectified in future editions.

© 2011 Kristi Fowler
ISBN 978-0-9840304-2-2

Kristi Fowler, LMFT, LLC
140 River Vista Place
Twin Falls, Idaho 83301

Dedicated to those of you who experienced tragedy, searching to find a way through...

Contents

Acknowledgements

This journey starts first with my family – my parents Jim and Jean and my sisters Kim and Jamie. Because of the story we have lived, the counsel offered in this book is very real, very personal and very passionate. Thank you, family, for letting me share with the world our family traumas so that others might be helped. To each of you...

Mom... you have the biggest heart of anyone I know. You are very giving, compassionate and loving. You are constantly volunteering. I will never forget how you went back to work full-time after being a "stay-at-home-Mom" for several years (since we were born) to help pay for the medical bills our family had accumulated. You are truly a person of sacrifice, willing to give what you have to make all of our lives better. You wanted all of us girls to get what you did not. You made sure we went to college and received an education. I admire your faith and how you have leaned on it to get you through tough times. I love you tremendously.

Dad... you have always been my encourager. You encouraged me to go beyond my limitations even when life's events seemed to indicate otherwise. You are someone who would give the shirt off his back in order to help someone out. The amount of time, money and labor you have given to people is staggering. But that's what you do and I appreciate it. You have owned your own business all these years and survived through the various tragedies that have come our way. I love your direct and honest approach. Your work ethic is second to none.

To my sisters... There really is something to sisterhood. We have gone through so much together. I appreciate our friendship tremendously, even during those times I didn't like hearing what you had to say. I know that you both love me and I hope you know how much I love the both of you.

Kim... you are a true testament to overcoming the odds. You undertook the challenge of finding a "new normal" for your life and did so with tremendous success. You graduated from high school and college after being told you would never be able. You are a motivational speaker invited to speak at university campuses and other organizations regarding the grueling journey from burn victim to burn survivor. You volunteer at countless causes for burn organizations, including serving on national and regional boards. You volunteer at your church, raise money for kids to attend burn camps, and do re-entry activities for kids going back to school after burn tragedies. You do all of this while being a wonderful mother to two great kids. I admire you as my sister, but also as a woman. Your love, perseverance and compassion make you an amazing person.

Jamie... you are much the same way. You have pushed yourself to the top of your profession, earning a PhD and serving as a college professor. You are an athletic trainer as well, helping athletes reach their maximum potential. You, too, volunteer at your church and in your community, carrying on the tradition set forth by our parents. You are a wonderful wife and mother of three girls. I admire your inner drive and healthiness which inspires all the members of our family.

A very special thanks to Steve and Nancy Fowler for their editing that contributed greatly to the final product. Your feedback and insights were spot on and I am grateful for your intricate care in helping me with this project.

Several individuals contributed to the process of reviewing and offering suggestions to improve the manuscript – Debbie Lund, Becky Elam, Dan and Sonja Willie, Gary and Jeannie Wolverton, Lonette Brown, Lezlie Matthews, Trudy Dane, Monica Matthews, Dyne Peich, Con Paulos, and Bryan Matsouka. My gratitude extends to all of you for taking the time to invest yourself in the pages of this book. I appreciate your encouragement and thoughtfulness as you took great care in helping the process.

A very special thank you goes to my clients for whom I was inspired to write this book. Thank you for the privilege of entering your "story" and working together to help you get the most out of this life.

To my kids, Cody and Kendra... As your Mom, I hope to give you as much as you have given me. You are both terrific people, full of potential and I could not be more proud.

And lastly to my husband, Sam... You are the most loving and patient man I know. I never could have done this without you.

Kristi Fowler
Twin Falls, Idaho

Author's Note

I come to you through the pages of this book as a counselor who has been privileged to have sat with many clients going through tragedy. That, combined with my own experiences of trauma – and those of my family – lead me to give you an honest portrayal of life in the wake of tragedy. A couple of things about that... First, it may hit too close to home for you if you are still reeling from your own personal tragedy. I completely understand. Feel free to skip to tangible hints and helps when you cannot take reading a story that hits close to home.

Second, I want to define two words you will hear throughout the book. I mention the idea of the "injured." What I mean by "injured" are the people who have been afflicted physically as a result of a tragedy. They were the ones physically "hurt." There are several different instances of what that could mean... illness, disease, broken bones and body, burns, etc. It also entails the concepts of those stricken with a diagnosis or the revelation of a genetic defect. It also includes those who have suffered abuse or a violent assault on their person. If you could imagine all of the possible ways a person could be "injured," that is what I mean to include in that word.

The other word is "non-injured." These are the people affected by the trauma, but have no physical afflictions as a result. They weren't the ones "hurt." They don't have the physical scars, wounds, broken bones, disease, illness, abuse, etc. However, as you will read, their experience of tragedy is just as profound.

Thirdly, I am going to share about my feelings/actions/thoughts and those of my clients, parents and siblings. When it comes to my family it is important to note, these are my memories. I am incredibly grateful for my family. We lived our tragedies together. We did the best we knew how. We did some things well and other things not so well. We have been through quite a bit and enjoy our days now as people who have seen "the other side" of tragedy. It behooves me to tell you the honest truth about that with which we struggled in hopes that you can avoid some of the pitfalls we discovered.

And so... read this knowing that there is "the other side" and our family has been blessed to find its way there. I bring to light our mistakes or regrets for no other reason than a convictional belief that in doing so, you and yours can be helped. For the Calman (my maiden name) clan, that's what it has always been about... helping others. And so, I hope this book helps you. We would love nothing more than nudging you toward a journey that results in redemption and meaning. And I hope you get to experience that "better story" that I have come to enjoy and appreciate with my family.

Because... you deserve it.

Kristi (Calman) Fowler
July 2011

Introduction

Have you ever stood in the ocean marveling at the scenery, when all of a sudden... a wave knocks you off your feet?

You get soaked, you fall backwards and you desperately hold your breath as the wave passes over you. As you struggle to get back on your feet and regain your balance, you wipe your eyes just in time to see... the next wave coming at you.

Before you know it, you are on your back again, fighting to find your way to the surface. You gulped in a mouthful of salty seawater on the way down and you feel as if this wave has you "pinned." Panic starts to set in, and you scramble to the surface, gasping for air.

And there it is... another wave coming your way.

And another...

And another...

Sometimes, it seems that the waves never stop pounding.

Given that this book is in your hands, I know you now understand life on a whole new level. Tragedy has struck. You've been hit by it, you've been wounded by it, and you have been trapped by it. I'm not sure where you are in the process, but I would assume that you are still in the midst of your nightmare, somehow searching for a way through the mess and madness that has invaded your life.

Tragedy. Trauma. Crisis.

The grief... the pain... the heartache... the loss... My hunch is, the thought "How could this happen?" has raced through your heart and head more than a few times.

The unthinkable. The unbelievable. The unimaginable.

Sometimes, it seems that the waves never stop pounding.

People off the coast of Sumatra, Indonesia took such a pounding on December 26, 2004. An earthquake registering 9.2 on the Richter scale occurred underwater, unleashing one of the deadliest natural disasters in history. When all was said and done, over 230,000 people died in the countries of Indonesia, Sri Lanka, India and Thailand. As wave after wave entered shallow water and began to amplify on shore, thousands of people were sent in search of higher ground only to be engulfed by nature's latest roar. Massive debris, shattered buildings, families thrown into immediate crisis... the signs were everywhere of total devastation. It was "trauma" on a large scale. The unleashed powers of nature had instantly transformed thousands, if not millions of lives. Nothing would ever be the same for people in those countries. And the truth is, those of us watching around the world on television would never be the same, either.

"Trauma" is like that (I am using the word "trauma" throughout the book to capture the idea of "tragedy," "crisis," "illness," "diagnosis," "the worst news ever," "unexpected event," etc.). Especially "event" trauma, in which an incident occurs that launches everything from its own epicenter. It swoops in, demands its due and leaves just as quickly. Or so it seems. The footprints of such a trauma do not actually fade from the sand quite as easily. The event awakens emotions and thoughts typically vaulted in the subconscious – fear, anxiety, hardship, change, trust. And, just as the trauma unfolds with force, so do the after-effects. Things that didn't seem issues, all of a sudden, are huge. The minute abilities we commonly take for granted appear to take on a new life, leaving us ravaged from the toll that even the "normal" extracts.

Wave after wave after wave...

A tsunami is a great metaphor for tragedy. The trauma that results – both the event and the after-affects – feels very much like wave after wave pounding your "shore."

Those waves hurt. They pile on top of you. And they keep coming.

I remember watching with millions of others the events that transpired in the 2004 Indonesian tsunami. A friend who was tuned into the 'blog-o-sphere' kept my husband and me up to speed with "eye on the ground reports." I remember news organizations daily upping the number of victims, lending more and more significance to the awesome force with which the tsunami hit shore. There was the constant search for something "good" – the child rescued from a mass of rubble... the family reunited after having been split up in the disaster... the heroic people who risked their own lives to save someone else. I remember feeling – as I did with other event traumas that have happened during my life (9/11, New Orleans, Mt. St. Helens, to name a few) – incredible pain, sadness, relief, and compassion.

While the effect on my TV screen wasn't anywhere near to what someone on the ground in Indonesia was experiencing, I got the picture: ***When "trauma" hits, it hits hard. And fast. It is unrelenting***.

More recently, the tsunami that hit Japan in March of 2011 brought back all of those same feelings, thoughts and fears.

You know those feelings.

You know those thoughts.

You know those fears.

Wave after wave after wave...

Tsunami.

Here's what I have lived as a human being and what I know as a professional therapist who deals with people's tragedies on a daily basis: ***the trauma doesn't stop when the "event" is over.*** It doesn't end when you leave the hospital. The event begins the trauma and catapults it into an even greater force... a tsunami. Even though the devastation of the event is incredibly painful, gut-wrenching and near impossible to fathom; the weeks, months and years that follow can be worse if there is not intentional care of the situation. The decisions people make (especially those "in charge"), the behaviors people engage, and the attitudes/beliefs they walk away with have everything to do with whether the trauma "wins" or not.

The tragedy can become *THE* story or it can become a *PIECE* of the story.

If all you consider is the negative effects, your tsunami "wins." Please hear me... that is not to make light of the disaster. It was truly horrific. I wouldn't wish it on anyone. But, it is also possible to consider that the tsunami may have produced some positive things ***without denying the devastation that took place***. If devastation is the end of the story –

if it becomes THE story – then we miss the point. We miss the power within us to *redeem* something. That is, to take something "bad" and make something "good" come out of it without minimizing the event, without over-simplifying or over-spiritualizing the event, and without denying the affects of the event.

Is it possible that something "good" could come out of this?

Is it possible that this could lead you to live a better story?

Is it possible that you could find new meaning and purpose from all that has happened?

When the unthinkable happens, we just want to shut down. Often, it is too big, too overwhelming, too taxing… We want to quit. We want to forget it and just "exist," whatever "exist" is. But to do so denies the human spirit. To do so denies human resiliency. To do so lets the tragedy win…

Here's the deal: tragedy happens. And often, there is no rhyme or reason why. The question is, who is going to win? You? Or the tragedy?

The "trauma tsunami" most certainly has negative effects. However, it is possible for it to have positive effects as well. It all comes down to how people choose to respond. Are they aware of the "waves" that continue to roll in as a result of the experience? Do they know which waves are destructive? Do they know there are good waves to catch along the way? Are they prepared with information to know what could happen or what is normal to expect? Are they adequately able to develop new coping skills? Are they aware of the unspoken and subconscious messages that pound their brains? Is a person able to adjust to what is happening with the others around them – even as they are attending to their own "stuff" from the trauma? Does a person know what waves can catapult them to success in dealing with what has taken place? All of these questions and more are crucial in understanding how to respond to the trauma that has rocked your world.

How you choose to respond is <u>*everything*</u>.

As one whose family or loved ones have experienced a deep, wounding trauma from some sort of unpredictable or unplanned event (or set of circumstances), you get it. In fact, you might be in the midst of it right now. If so… this book is for you. Trust me, the tragedy you have been through or are currently going through is every bit as life-changing and unsettling as the Indian Ocean tsunami of 2004. Because you are in the midst of it, you may be wondering how to respond to all of this. Your "radar" that normally discerns what is healthy and unhealthy may have been thrown out of whack by the "unthinkable" that has occurred. You are probably exhausted, mentally and physically drained, and somewhat embarrassed you couldn't figure out how to avoid the unpredictable in the first place.

All of these and more are normal reactions to the unimaginable happening. I want to help you find your way in your situation, understand what is really going on within you and around you, and give you the tools that best help prepare you to engage the lingering effects.

The tragedy doesn't have to be the last chapter in your story... My hope is that, for you, it is a catapult to a much better story.

I know that sounds crazy. But the fact you are reading this means that your life has been turned upside down. Frankly, you are probably not sure how or if you are going to make it. Perhaps, you might not even be sure you want to. This is a book about that. It bluntly tells the truth on how tragedy affects the family. It addresses the waves of the resulting tsunami that continue to crash your shoreline.

While much has been written on what life is like for the "injured", much less has been written for the "rest of the family" to understand what happens to them. If a child in the family is critically hurt in an accident and has life forever altered, what about the parents? What about the other children? Did they not "experience" the tragedy, too? How does the act of parenting change? How does the family system adapt? How does the trauma affect the behaviors of the other kids in the family? What of the guilt and shame associated with the event that all in the family carry with them?

Tsunami.

The images that come to mind simply mentioning the word give you an idea of what I mean by "family trauma tsunami."

The Indonesian tsunami of 2004 did not end when the ocean calmed down and waves rolled back into the sea – and neither did your "tsunami." You have had effects you could never have predicted – and perhaps more to come. You are experiencing feelings, pain, and conflict you never realized would be there. You are fighting to survive, awash in a sea of waves, hoping that the nightmare will someday end before it becomes a part of who you are. It is why the idea of "tsunami" is a good one to understand. A tsunami isn't one big tidal wave... it is a series of waves that keep crashing in on you.

But, the ocean isn't just the place where tsunamis lie in wait. The ocean is much more than that. Truth be told, most of the waves in the ocean are meant to be enjoyed, whether through a scenic beach view, sailing across the water or on top of a surfboard going for a great ride. The key is understanding the waves themselves... how they break, the variations in the sets as they roll in, and the way they weave and move in the sea. Some waves have destructive force written all over them. Others are the exact pathways to a great ride across the sea.

And so, the metaphor sets up like this: there are waves worth catching and there are waves worth avoiding. Trauma launches you into all sorts of things, good and bad. However, where you land is up to you. When surfing the ocean, where you go – whether you end up pinned underneath gasping for air or smoothly gliding along the surface carving a beautiful wake – depends on two things: reading the waves and choosing the one that gives you the best ride.

In the pages that follow, I will tell you about the waves – how to recognize them, pay attention to them, which waves to ride and which ones to avoid. How you choose to ride is up to you...

CHAPTER ONE

Finding My Way

A person tends to remember vividly the first moment in her life that time stood still. For most, it is the moment you first saw that special someone. Or, that first hit in a baseball game, the first good report card, or the first time you knew you made your parents proud.

Exciting, positive and the thrill of accomplishment – all traits of a "time stood still" moment...

Not mine.

The day started easily enough. My family was headed to a friend's house for dinner. I was excited. Not only were they great company, but my friend's mother was a fabulous cook. I couldn't wait to taste some of her terrific desserts. The day was September 15, 1984. I was thirteen. When we arrived we did the usual socializing – food, games and hang out time. There was a fire going in the pit that Todd (20) and Evan (14) were tending. Todd told me to go get my older sister (and his girlfriend), Kim (17). I ran into the house, got her and we went outside. As we walked up to the fire, we saw Evan pouring some diesel on the fire at Todd's insistence. Just then... the can exploded.

And for a moment... time stood still.

It was like an M-80 firecracker had exploded. The bomb-like blast was the can exploding in two, sending off a big ball of fire that hit Evan's legs in one direction and Kim's and Todd's faces in the other. Right then, it felt as if everything went into slow motion. Evan leaned his face back in time so the ball of fire missed his face, and as he did he doused me with the remaining diesel in the can. Jamie (11) and Evan's little sister had been standing by a tree right behind Kim when the blast occurred and they bolted toward the house. Everything was so real, and yet, so unreal. "This can't really be happening," was my thought. It felt as if we were in a movie, running at slow speed. My thirteen-year-old mind didn't know how to respond, so I did what thirteen-year-olds do when they panic: I laughed.

As I spun round and round to put out the fire that had latched onto my ankle, my frozen moment in time was shattered by Evan's piercing screams. "I'm on fire! I'm on fire!" Instantly, what had once felt like slow motion now became a blur of reality. My first instinct was to jump on Evan's legs and smother the flames with my body. For some reason, I didn't. Instead, I fell to my knees and started pounding his legs with my hands to get the fire out. I later learned that jumping on him would have made flames immediately engulf me, given the diesel that had been spilled on me.

My Dad came running out of the house, saw Evan, and ran over to us. In one motion, he yanked Evan's pants off his body. Not able to shed my 8th grade reality, I remember thinking, "Wow... I've never seen a boy in his underwear before!" Why I thought that I have no idea. Shock does weird things to you.

We extinguished the flames on Evan. Then Jamie saw my sister Kim and grabbed Dad to show him. She had rolled up against the back tire of a truck – just lying there face down on fire. Right then, Evan's mom came out of the house with blankets. We grabbed them to put out the flames that were ravaging her body.

And then... silence. Time stood still again. It was like we all were standing there catching our collective breath, when out of nowhere... Todd. He was walking like he was drunk, with arms raised, and from his waist up he was one solid flame. Evan's mom and I ran up to him, pounding him as hard as we could to get the flames out. My Dad ran and tackled him, knocking us down as well. I was so glad he was face down. He had no hair, nose, ears or fingers left. His body had been devoured by flames, resembling charcoal. He lifted his head and said, "My hair is gone, isn't it?" That freaked me out.

The scene was one of sheer disbelief. Panic was everywhere.

I ran to the house and dialed 911. I remember it felt like forever until 911 answered the phone. It seemed like years before the ambulance arrived. Once it did, my world became a blur. All I could keep saying was, "How could this happen?"

Once the ambulance arrived, the paramedics took over. In the midst of utter shock, I took notice of one particular sight. A single shoe was sitting nearby, still on fire. My Dad walked up and kicked the shoe as hard as he could. He had the look of total failure... helpless, powerless, and completely defeated.

An earthquake had just triggered our tsunami.

Between the time the ambulance left and prior to understanding the gravity of what had taken place a short time later, I allowed myself to believe that this was just "an accident." Accidents are like broken arms – you get them, they heal and life moves on without a radical adjustment in your story. Even at the hospital, I responded like the teenager I was. "When can we go home?" I would ask. "Can't we leave now? Can't they just send Kim home?" I soon learned this wasn't a "broken arm" scenario. It wasn't just a simple accident – this was life and death. And it was life and death for a solid month for my sister.

Kim, Todd, and Evan were all taken to the regional burn center at the University of Washington Harborview Medical Center in Seattle, WA, one hundred miles south of our home. Todd would die ten days later due to his extreme burns. It was revealed that Kim had 65% of her body burned and had to undergo 95 days of intensive treatment in the hospital. "Intensive"… that word doesn't begin to describe the agony she endured. I felt horrified every time I walked through the doors of the hospital not being able to even identify my own sister.

This was a horror movie. "The Fire" as it came to be known in our family, had changed our lives forever. As a thirteen-year-old sitting by my sister's bed, all I could think about was, "Why wasn't it me?" I hadn't been badly burned. Why not? "It should have been me," I would tell myself over and over. I was the one who ran into the house to get my sister. If I hadn't listened to Todd, this never would have happened to her. She never would have been in this place if it weren't for me. I felt guilty. I felt responsible. I felt… lucky. And I felt wrong for feeling that way…

Life changed. The recovery process for Kim was long and torturous. Twenty-five operations. Amputated thumb and ear. Every day for her was an exercise in pain that was beyond excruciating. My mother lived during the week at Kim's side, not knowing whether her daughter would live or die. My father took his turn on weekends, after spending the week trying to make ends meet for the family. Truth be told, life changed for my parents in ways I could never have imagined as a thirteen-year-old. I understand that so much more now as an adult and parent. Looking back, I am incredibly grateful for all my parents had to do to get our family through this event.

Bad things happen to good people. Every single day, tragedy happens in people's lives who have always had the right intentions. That was certainly the case with us. This was no one's "fault." My parents, Evan, Todd, my sister, me... we are all good people. Mistakes take place all the time.

In the weeks to come, my sister Jamie and I adjusted to life at home, taking on roles and responsibilities previously tended to by our mother. The toll took its effect on everyone... Kim, Mom, Dad, Jamie, me. Life would never be the same.

The wave of exhaustion crashed in on us.

The wave of rage and fear crashed in on us.

The wave of the unknown crashed in on us.

Sometimes, it seems that the waves never stop pounding.

We had to find a "new normal".

But I still wanted life "the way it used to be." I was holding onto my fantasy when Kim came home on Dec. 19, 1984. Finally, we could be a family again. But the fantasy was shattered quickly. That happens when every day starts with crying and screaming as my Mom would help Kim put on her compression garments. Kim's pain was intolerable. She was faced with the damage to her body every single day. She faced returning to school and adjusting to classmates who were adjusting to her. She faced rehabilitation and the mental stress of learning how to do things she once took for granted. She faced fears, doubts, pain, anger... and the constant wonder if life would ever be good again.

I wondered the same thing.

The stress of our new reality was evident everywhere. My mom was exhausted. My father was, too. Jamie and I would feel the heaviness of their exhaustion as we witnessed their longing for a life that once was and a guilt that ate at them constantly. They were doing everything they could for their family and yet, feeling like they hadn't done enough.

Life wasn't any easier for Jamie and me dealing with Kim. We bore the brunt of Kim's rage as she struggled to find a new identity amidst her pain. We knew her rage was understandable, yet we were tired of it. We wanted life back to "normal." It was in the middle of those times I remember thinking, "I wish she was back in the hospital." I felt so ashamed for thinking that. And yet, it was honest.

I was caught between a rock and a hard place. My beliefs and feelings conflicted with each other and I felt ashamed of them all.

"The Fire" happened to me. And it didn't. I began to come to grips with the reality that my life was forever changed, yet I wasn't the "victim." "The Fire" changed my life, yet I had no external scars to see. It left me in a very, very strange place. I felt both guilty and relieved at the same time. How do you honor your own feelings about what happened to you when nothing really happened to you? Who are you when you are now just a sideshow in your own family? How do you own your own guilt for being healthy and able? How do you handle it when you lose your own identity so a person you love can recover hers? Should a person feel mad about that? Should I feel guilty for being mad? I was scarred, but I wasn't burned. I existed in a place that had no definition... that had no voice. I was lost. I felt I had no rights.

My family had the same issues. We were angry over the situation, but we had no way of processing it or talking about it. We didn't even know if we had the right to feel angry. At the time, being angry was not something that was accepted in our various community circles. We needed to be "okay" with everything. At least, that's the stance we took so as to honor our belief system.

But the anger was there.

Wave after wave of things to be angry about rolled in... Kim's never-ending pain... how unfair it was... life being totally disrupted... our frustration with each other... the "why" questions... miscommunication... the doubts we had about the future.

Then, out of nowhere, the wave we weren't expecting crashed on our shore. Prior to the day of "The Fire" my parents were in the process of changing insurance companies. In the transition, it was discovered that there was a day or two that our family wasn't covered. The day of "The Fire" happened to be one of those days.

The bills piled up to a staggering amount of money.

Tsunami.

We undercommunicated and overspiritualized to cope. It's what we knew. And we continued to live... or exist... or whatever it was that we did. All three sisters dealt with it our own way. Kim was the victim. I became the overfunctioning good girl. Jamie rebelled. Dad worked more. Mom worried and prayed more. Life became a walk through time echoing the silence of shattered innocence. Never again would I believe that being "good" kept you safe. "Safe" was a long time ago, left with a child who was no more...

Trauma. It hits hard and it is unrelenting.

I share this with you not so you will feel sorry for me or my family. I doubt that what my family went through is much different than what you are going through right now. I do want you to know this, though... **You are not the only ones to have gone through times like these and you are not alone.** There is a whole world of us out there who can relate to everything you are experiencing.

"Event" trauma, such as the tsunami that hit the Indian Ocean or "The Fire" in my family, is unpredictable. You don't know when it is going to occur. You don't plan for it. Why would you? You are never fully prepared when it takes place – despite your best intentions. Frankly, a person doesn't normally consider that such a thing would happen to him. Who hopes for that? The concept of "unpredictability" makes event trauma its own unique entity in the field of trauma study. And truthfully, it happens much more than we think.

While natural disasters of the magnitude we've been discussing are well known, less known are the event traumas that families encounter all the time... the child who is severely injured... the house that burns to the ground... the sexual abuse of a sibling... the car accident that critically wounds a parent... the moment you were told your child has leukemia... when you heard the doctor say, "tumor" or "diabetes"... the ultrasound revealing your baby has a birth defect... the flames that burn your sister.

If you have been through such an unpredictable event in your life, you understand. This is different. It hits hard and fast and leaves long-lasting effects. And when it hits... a person's whole world collapses. Life is now different. Attitudes are different. Attending to the simple and mundane is different. Nothing feels safe, nothing feels normal, and nothing feels predictable anymore. It makes a person wonder if his world was ever really all that safe in the first place.

Sometimes, it seems that the waves never stop pounding.

CHAPTER TWO

Finding Your Way in a Tsunami

First off, let me say this. You can make it through this, if you choose.

You have what it takes.

You are strong enough, smart enough and resilient enough to persevere through your tragedy, and you can come out on "the other side" even better than you were before.

I know those words are probably hard to believe – and may even sound infuriating at the moment – but I want you to know that they are true. I have worked with countless families who have been through tough times and have been through enough tragedy myself to know that you WILL get through this.

If you choose to embrace what has happened, you CAN come out even better.

I have learned that these times in life not only change us, but change us in ways that can be great. I know how hard that must be to hear – there was a time in my life when I didn't believe these words, either. I have seen it over and over in the lives of my clients. Please hear me – I am NOT saying that I am glad this happened to you. I am not saying that at all. What I am saying is that what has taken place (or continues to take place) can bring out good things in you that you never knew were there.

I love to hear Bethany Hamilton's attitude and words regarding what happened to her and the shark attack she suffered while surfing one day. That shark attack caused her to lose an arm, something tragic – especially for a competitive surfer. In "Soul Surfer," the movie that told her story, a scene takes place at the end of a surf meet where her character is asked by a reporter, "If you could go back to that day and not have gone surfing, would you do it?" She responds, "I wouldn't change what happened to me, because then I wouldn't have this chance in front of all of you to embrace more people than I could ever have with two arms." That's the exact attitude about which I am speaking.[1]

Some of the things you are encountering will actually help you live a better story than the one you had been living up until this point. There is hope to be found in the midst of all this, and I want you to hear that from me in a very profound way right from the start. While you may not see light at the end of the tunnel today, you can trust me that the light is out there waiting for you. I have lived it, I have worked with it and I know some great people who have used what has happened to make a difference.

---

[1] Soul Surfer, dir. Sean McNamara, perf. AnnaSophia Robb, Film District, TriStar Pictures, 2011.

Believe me when I say that, in the journey you are going through... there is hope, there is life, and there is healing awaiting you...

Understanding a Tsunami

The first step in your journey toward getting a grasp on all of this is understanding the nature of how trauma works. If it were like a tidal wave, you would have one mammoth event and the seas would grow calm again. There would be devastation, but the waves would cease to continue. A tsunami is not a one-wave-and-you-are-done event. What makes tsunamis unique is that they bring wave after wave after wave until the sea settles – and those waves can each act like their own tidal wave.

For example, perhaps your family member was in a serious accident and rushed to the hospital. After not knowing initially, you found out that your loved one will live. Some surgeries need to take place, but you have found hope once again. The surgeries begin and all of a sudden... infection hits. That infection leads to more tests where the possibilities are presented to you on what could happen. Some sound great and some sound downright scary. Again, you find yourself unsure of where this will all lead. That unknown scares you deeply. The family chooses a course of action after weighing the options which leads to another gut-wrenching surgery. The surgery goes well. But, that is followed by a new round of medication. And maybe your family member doesn't respond well to those meds. You discover the family member is going to need on-going care. And now you are behind at work, the boss is calling and you feel torn. Your bills are piling up and they need to be paid.

And so on and so on...

The waves just keep coming.

Tsunami.

A tsunami actually begins with an earthquake. It is what triggers everything else. Your accident, sudden news, or shocking new reality (cancer, heart defect, etc.) is just like the earthquake. It's the "event" that puts everything else in motion. It sets up the waves to start rolling in.

"Trauma" comes with waves that continue to pound your shore, beginning with the original event.

The wave of disbelief.

The wave of confusion.

The wave of reality.

The wave of intense rage.

The wave of the unknown future.

The wave of... You get the idea.

Here's the thing: an earthquake in a tsunami also brings to light forces that were already at play – tetonic plates bumping into each other causing friction, environmental factors, ill-preparedness in certain systems and structures, and the underlying beliefs and attitudes that people had about what could ever really happen to them.

Not unlike this phenomena in a tsunami, is your ordeal. Things that were already at play in your life might now rise to the surface. They will be exposed as the tragedy hits home and as the waves keep rolling in. Some of those things that are exposed may not feel very good. In fact, you might feel ashamed, embarrassed or even horrified that certain thoughts, feelings, and habits have been exposed, whether it be in your marriage, parenting, family rules, etc. On the other hand, it might also unearth some really neat elements of your loved ones and you, bringing a sense of calm and peace.

It is important to remember that this is all part of it. And while the damage may be vast, the story does not end there.

If we take to heart the tsunami analogy, we can take refuge in the knowledge of what is bound to come. While you may not know in advance the details of every wave that crashes your shore, understanding that they are coming takes some of the "surprise" element away. And that, itself, is helpful. Being blindsided is never fun, which is why taking notice of the likelihood of certain waves rolling in brings an element of confidence back to us. It's the not knowing that often makes the struggle even harder. Anticipating that more is to come – even if you don't know the details – prepares you to meet those challenges head on. My hope is that it normalizes what is happening so you don't feel crazy or confused and then simply react.

Is It Really That Big a Deal?

I've had clients who have asked me that before. They want to know if what they've experienced is really all that big a deal compared to what others go through. They see things like the Idonesian Tsunami or the hurricane that hit New Orleans and minimize their experiences. They hear the stories of others and automatically assume that their situations pale in comparison. Are their crises really that big?

How do you know if you have been touched by trauma? You may be thinking, "Well... it didn't really happen to me. After all, I'm not the one who got hurt." Or, "I only saw it... It's not like I experienced it." Or, "I wasn't around when it happened. I only heard the story..." Or, "What happened to me is not as bad as what happened to _____."

You may find yourself explaining away feelings, thoughts, or attitudes that all of a sudden have emerged in your life. You may attempt to logically reason that "stuff like this" happens to everyone. You may also argue the opposite – "stuff like this" is supposed to happen to "someone like me." After all, "I deserve it." You may experience anger, grief, pain, distrust, confusion, hostility, passivity, aloneness, fright, numbness, or discontent. You may be doing everything in your power to "keep things normal." You might even deny that anything has taken place to cause any of these ideas, thoughts and feelings within you. You may find moments where you are asking, "Did this really happen?"

If any of this rings true in your heart and mind, you have experienced trauma. And, to answer the initial question, "yes," it is a big deal. Please understand, though... all of these – and more – are normal reactions to what has transpired in your life.

A traumatic event can be caused by any number of things. For most people, the actual event that took place – accident, abuse, heart defect, cancer, etc. – only begins to open up more doors that make "trauma" an on-going, active cycle of living. What you are dealing with is more than just the event that took place – it is the effects of the event physically, psychologically, emotionally, spiritually.

That is why it is so important to understand the nature of trauma... *Trauma is not a one-time thing.* It is not a singular event that can be quickly swept under the rug in the attempt to "move on" with life. If you attempt to "move on" too soon, the effects can become even more devastating as time goes on. Too often in our need to find "normal" again, we short-circuit the process of dealing with tragedy.

My first caution to you in understanding trauma is this: Don't minimize it. It did not end when the actual event stopped. Your dealing with it should not end there either.

I often hear this in my office: "Shouldn't I be done dealing with this? When will this be over?" This is often a coping mechanism used by people to bypass what is really going on inside. It is an attempt to "forget about it" which actually works against the person creating that belief.

A good measure to go by is this... If it has been more than a year since your unthinkable event took place and you are still struggling with it the way you did in the beginning, then you may not have dealt with that which is really hurting you. In light of that, seeing a counselor or professional who can help you identify what is really going on is a very smart and beneficial thing to do.

It is crucial to understand initially that everyone *reacts to tragedy differently*. There is not a standard set of "rules" that apply across the board to people who have experienced the unimaginable. This is due to stage of development as a human being, previous experiences, personality, coping skills, conditioned beliefs, faith, and the support system a person may or may not have.

Some people bury trauma. Other people can't stop talking about it. Some want to turn it into a bigger drama and others just constantly wish the whole thing never happened. Gender plays a role... men and women experience tragedy differently. The other children in your household may experience what you have been through differently than you or their siblings.

The goal of this book is to give you understanding of how trauma affects each of us and how to prepare yourself for encountering it as it weaves its way into your family story.

"Yeah, BUT..."

Okay... you've been reading for awhile. You've heard the argument for how vital it is to pay attention to trauma and what is really happening. I'm guessing that, at some point in the last few pages you have muttered the words, "Yeah... but..." Trust me, I get it. I understand. There is something unique about your story, and what I have begun to tell you needs to be understood in light of *your* experience, *your* story, *your* situation. And you know what? You're right.

However...

Let me "Yeah, but..." with your thoughts for a second. Tragedy makes all of us ask "Why me? What did I do to deserve this?" When we begin to contemplate the answers to those questions it leads us down a path that ends in the shaming of ourselves and others. Before long, we can thoroughly believe that the trauma is a direct result of our words (or lack thereof), our actions (or lack thereof), and *who we are as a person.*

I have news for you: You did nothing to deserve this. Nothing. If you are reading this as a parent of an injured child, that is very hard to hear. But please hear me... In addition, do not fall for the words of others who knowingly or unknowingly say words to make you feel like it is all your fault. Do not get stuck in that place... This is not all your fault. Staying trapped there does not allow you to help you, your spouse or your child over the journey on which you should be embarking.

The shame message "it's all my fault" is unproductive. What has happened, has happened. There is nothing you can do to undo it... you can only move on from here and find a way to make the best of it.

Let me sidebar here for a moment, since it is entirely possible that you read the last paragraph and said, "But you don't get it... I AM the one who caused the unthinkable to take place!" Maybe you were the drunk driver... Maybe you were the one who fell asleep at the wheel... Maybe you were the one who lit the match that set the fire... Maybe you are the one who carries the gene for heart problems...

Without going into a long psychological explanation, let me just say this: Shame is going to eat at you in a way that you have never experienced previously. And, even though you caused the event, you need to know that toxic shame still has no place. Shame will try to get you to forever punish yourself for your decision, choice or mistake. Don't buy the lie. Yes, you have consequences with which you may have to deal, and those may even add to the shame message. But I am here to tell you that toxic shame won't help you in the long run. The situation you have created (or helped create) will be healed ultimately by your willingness to accept what you did, make the right amends for what has happened and pursue being a better person as a result of your healing efforts. And while a millstone around your neck for the rest of your days may seem suitable self-inflicted punishment, you need to understand that it won't ever help you feel better.

We live better stories and become better people when we stare our shortcomings in the face and own them... that is, turning around and walking 180 degrees in the opposite direction, never to return to being the person who allowed himself to be the trigger of the tragedy. You deal with it, own it, and deal with the consequences of it without letting it become the definer of who you are. Then, hopefully, one day you will look back at your journey and find yourself thankful for having been restored... and a better person for it.

Beating the Shame Game

Look... no matter what your role is in your current family crisis, I understand. There is nothing I – or you – can say to take the pain away.

I really do understand.

But... If you are feeling the need to stay "stuck" in the shame place, let me ask you this: What are you trying to accomplish? How is that going to change anything? By focusing on your guilt, you only paralyze yourself and are unable to help anyone. If you stay stuck in that place you will damage your marriage, your relationship with your kids and the friendships with those around you. You will actually create the very things you are hoping to avoid.

While crisis helps create fertile soil for the shame game, you cannot allow it to win. You deserve better than that, your family deserves better than that and the injured person in this story deserves better than that. There is hope around the corner....

You already know this is not going to be easy.

But you <u>must</u> challenge yourself.

You must believe in you.

You can do this...

CHAPTER THREE

Finding Your Way Through The Trauma Maze

Let me tell you some things that trauma most definitely is...

Trauma is... in the eye of the beholder. Think, for a moment, about witnessing a fender-bender at a four-way stop in your town. You and a couple of others see it. As you wait for the police officer to arrive to fill out an accident report, you get to talking with the others. As you converse, you notice that all of you picked up on different parts of the story. All of you seemingly saw the same thing, but also, somehow, saw something different.

Trauma is exactly like that. What hits one person one way may hit another differently. The key is to understand and accept – in order for healing to take place – that any and all viewpoints are important to embrace as real.

Recently, I wrote an article for a magazine about my version of "The Fire" that took place in our family. It was interesting to hear back from my parents and sisters because they all had different versions of the story. Even more interesting, everyone had the belief that his or her version was the right one! *The truth is, it has nothing to do with being right or wrong about what actually happened. It has everything to do with how we experienced the event.*

When family members or friends begin to argue, defend, or justify their experiences, healing gets derailed and people can remain emotionally stuck for years. The important thing is that each person's story and experience is validated so that he or she can begin to heal from what he or she experienced.

Trauma is... the author of confusion and uncertainty. More than likely, people's first reactions to tragedy – once their mind goes "philosophical" – are, "How could this happen?" Or, "Why did this happen?" Please know, these questions are normal. But I offer up some caution to you... These questions can also be dangerous – especially when attempting to deal with them at the height of aftermath of the event. A tsunami is like that... when you feel like the wave is pelting you, your first instinct when you are able to breathe again is to try to make sense of it – as if making sense of it right after the initial moments of tragedy can ease your pain. That can be a dangerous trap. In many cases, the "why" of trauma is somewhat obvious: we live in a cause and effect world. When certain choices are made, certain consequences can result.

However, more often than not, the "why" of crisis is unknown or cloudy at best. When my clients ask, "Why did this happen?", they want a reason. They are trying to find meaning and purpose for this event happening. They are hoping the pain will lessen.

But think about it... is there an answer to the "Why?" question that would ever be good enough to justify the pain you feel? Of course not. In most cases, asking "why" can be a dead-end road. A better path is to begin looking for meaning and the bigger purpose – things that often take time. If you cannot find that right now because your situation looks so bleak, hold onto the hope that everything can be healed. Everything. It just takes time...

Trauma is... uniquely able to undermine trust. Especially for kids. Everything from the belief that "Bad things shouldn't happen to good people." to "How could God allow this?" to "Why me?" sow seeds of distrust following trauma.

Tragedy makes the world feel unsafe. When we feel unsafe, we withhold our trust. We recoil into a position of defense, keeping at arm's length anything that could possibly harm, hurt or destroy us. I've known many trauma survivors who report that simply going out in public to the grocery store was an exercise in trust. When your world is shaken to the core in the trauma tsunami, learning to trust is a whole new ballgame. Childhood innocence is lost... adulthood hope seems a distant memory.

Tragedy destroys trust with what you understand about the world – how it works, how it should work and your role in it. It sends the injured and non-injured alike into emotional, mental and spiritual chaos. I tell clients of mine who experience trauma that the opposite of trust is control. When we don't trust something or someone, we seek to control it or them. How often we attempt to do exactly that! That's a dangerous path to take because we do not ever really have control.

Trauma is... a great launching pad for unhealthy beliefs. Trauma often awakens beliefs within us that we never really encountered or expressed.

Beliefs about right and wrong.

Beliefs about good and evil.

Beliefs about hope and fear.

Beliefs about justice and injustice.

Beliefs about the universe and our place in it.

For example, I have seen religious folks who become even more zealot-like in their fervor over explaining the tragedy ("It's God's will"). I have also seen similar folks go completely the other way and lose their faith altogether. I would dare say that both reactions are dangerous.

Other beliefs can be challenged as well. I know people who believe that being a good person should prevent bad things from happening to them. I know others who believe crisis is a result of education and upbringing. I know people who believe that tragedy finds its way to those who dwell on the possibility of it. I know others who believe that making a big deal of it is wrong.

The beliefs we hold – about family, faith, life – can be severely tested by tragedy. However, over time, there is a possibility of a new, re-configured belief that was actually healthier than the one we held in the first place. For the trauma survivor, that becomes a wonderful wave to ride in calmer waters...

Can you identify any beliefs you might have that are being challenged?

Trauma is… a sower of powerlessness. Often after tragedy, people feel powerless and hopeless. People hate feeling that way so they attempt to find things that can make them feel powerful once again. I see this quite often when working with families who have experienced trauma. People try to compensate for the "powerless" feeling by doing things that make them feel powerful – enforcing rules, over-indulging their child, getting angry when they talk to doctors, making demands of the nurses, etc.

As humans, we want power and control. It seems that those things are woven into the fabric of who we are. And yet, at times… that pursuit drives us to behaviors and attitudes that seemingly make us feel "powerful" but they are really just mere shadows of that for which we hoped. They lead us down patterned roads of unhealthy behavior, all the while thinking we have regained that "control" that we so dearly covet. The challenge here is coming to terms with the fact we really are powerless at times. Other times, we can recognize that it is appropriate to use the measure of power we may possess (i.e. being an advocate for yourself and the injured).

The power paradigm is at play constantly in trauma. When a family has experienced a devastating accident, you can see families who now never allow the child "to be out of sight." They become overly protective, seeking to squash any and all possibilities of hurt for the child or loved one. Because of the powerless feeling from tragedy (i.e. Why couldn't I stop it or prevent it? Why wasn't I aware of it? I can't go through this again. If I only would have done…, etc.), people are in a rush to reclaim power in order to reclaim control.

However, too often, what they reclaim is not power, but a cheap imitation that leads to more crashing waves of the trauma tsunami. And... something important to note: Addiction is often the result of trauma because many are searching for a replacement for the power they feel they lost. Or, it becomes a way for people to soothe their pain. Alcoholism, sex, gambling, spending, exercise, food... the list of potential addictions goes on and on.

Trauma is... a great place for shame to reign. As I mentioned earlier, for many, many people, this is the toughest one. For starters, let me describe the difference between guilt and shame. Guilt is that feeling you have when you did something you know you should not have... the lie you told, the mean thing you said, the extra doughnut for breakfast this morning (☺). It is the little bell that goes off inside us when we know we are actively engaged in doing something that is not beneficial to us or others.

Shame is entirely different. Shame is that voice inside that whispers to us that we are not worth it or we "deserve" certain bad things because we are fundamentally flawed as people. Shame can be incredibly toxic in that it seeks to destroy our sense of self, convincing us that we cannot be loved, don't deserve the best and are incapable of anything else but suffering and pain. That is an extreme picture for sure, but that is the way shame works.

I have seen too many folks who have encountered the unthinkable then come to believe that, "This is for the sins of my past." Or, "I deserve this." Or, "God must have felt I needed to be punished." If you feel this – at all – I want to tell you something: It's a lie. Don't buy it. Not for one second. That may be hard to hear, but it needs to ring in your heart and mind.

Shame-based thinking zaps us of energy, consumes our life and creates in us people of doom and depression. A person can work really hard to make up for his shame and find in the end that it was just a bunch of wasted energy. The world doesn't need more lost attempts from those seeking to "make up" for something – it needs more and more redemptive stories of hope.

Recognizing Symptoms of Trauma

If those are things that trauma "is," then what are things that trauma does? What I mean is, how can you tell some of the symptoms of trauma so you know how to alert yourself to the traps it sets along the way? In my experience as a counselor, I have witnessed people who were so unaware of the symptoms that they continued each day to dig themselves into a deeper hole as a result of the tragedy. It is extremely important for you to recognize this in your spouse and children, as well, lest the family begin to fall into some of the pitfalls we have discussed already.

Here are some symptoms of trauma:

- *Re-experiencing the "event" in our mind and body*. This can be so real, that it is as if the whole thing is happening all over again. This can happen in our dreams or while we are awake. You might even feel it in certain places in your body. It is our mind and body's way of struggling with the traumatic event. Smells, time of day, sounds, anniversary of the event, etc. might trigger this in you.
- *Intense feelings of anger*. This might be manifest in feeling useless, powerless, or how unfair the whole thing is. It might

be displayed in angry outbursts or having a shorter fuse. It can even be seen in wanting or seeking revenge. The feeling of anger is powerful and intense and can give the illusion of being back in control.

- **Difficulty sleeping.** You can't fall asleep – or stay asleep -- perhaps for fear of having another nightmare or that you might relive the event. It may also occur from having been out of your normal routine for so long. Perhaps you are unable to turn your brain "off" and subsequently, spend more time thinking and worrying.

- **Emotional exhaustion.** You can't think clearly, you feel numb or you struggle to remember things. Your body can only take so much before it shuts down to protect you. You might find you cry all the time, even at silly things. Or, perhaps, you cannot cry at all. Emotional exhaustion can produce both results.

- **Loss of appetite.** You may feel like you aren't hungry, or you may neglect your own needs because you feel the need to give to everybody else during this time. We will address this more later, but it is important to note that taking care of YOU is of utmost importance during this time.

- **Avoidance issues.** Signs of avoidance may be: never wanting to talk about the tragedy, not wanting to go to the hospital, feeling numb, difficulty having strong feelings, losing interest in things that were important to you before the trauma, or feeling disconnected from those close to you or the world around you.

All of these symptoms are normal, but can be difficult to understand while you or a family member is experiencing them. Keep in mind that the nature of trauma is such that confusion can reign – whether in your own heart and mind or in the web of your family system. That is why it is important to recognize the signs and symptoms so you are not caught off guard.

It is never fun getting hit by a wave you never saw coming...

CHAPTER FOUR

Finding <u>YOUR</u> Way

This chapter is about the one thing that can help you cope with all of this:

YOU.

You MUST take care of YOU when the unthinkable hits. Being a person of good character, you are likely inclined to think of others first. Taking care of you doesn't seem right. You want to take care of your loved one who is hurting. You want to be there for the others who are hurting as a result of what has taken place. You want to manage the crisis, to wrestle back some form of control over life. And, you can do all of that – so long as you take care of YOURSELF.

On an airplane, when you listen to the instructions before the flight takes off, you will hear the attendant instruct parents to put on their oxygen mask first should the need arise. That's right... parents are asked to take care of themselves before attending to accompanying children. There is a reason for this: if you pass out from a lack of oxygen, your dependent child will surely die. It flies in the face of our initial instinct, which is, to first take care of the one who is depending on us. We often feel that "love" is doing exactly that. However, true love is taking care of yourself enough so you can give of yourself to someone else. When dealing with tragedy – as crazy as it may sound – you must apply your "oxygen mask" first before attending to the needs of those around you.

Your tragedy is already beyond what you could have ever imagined. It isn't just the event itself – as difficult as that is to take in – it's everything else: managing the daily matters of life that continue (work, bills, home, etc.), dealing with everyone else's needs and emotions over the event; taking care of those you love; interacting with doctors and medical staff; finding the right help; being there for the injured person you love; attending to your other children's on-going lives; keeping up with financial obligations; and somehow, someway, finding time to maybe eat, sleep or take a brisk walk – if such a thing were possible without feeling like "I can't do this." And all of that leads up to the moment when that someone manages to say the very thing you least need to hear... and the last little bit of gas in your tank runs out.

Overwhelming, isn't it? In fact, I would imagine that if you are in the middle of your situation right now, you are emotionally flooded just reading this, because you have been living it, day in and day out.

Take a minute. Breathe. It's okay.

There are lots of areas of your life into which the waters of this trauma will flow. That's the way it is with tsunamis: the constant pounding of wave after wave and the seeping of water into cracks and crevices of life suddenly produce a very weak and unstable infrastructure, leading to the collapse of what was once a strong foundation. What you are experiencing has the *potential* to do exactly that... but that doesn't have to be the case.

Good Waves to Help You Take Care of You

I want to help you turn your tsunami into a happy and productive day at the beach instead. The good waves of the ocean – the ones the surfers wait for – can be seen when you properly position yourself and your family during the midst of this crisis. And make no mistake: YOU have the ability to choose the waves that will enable you to prevail.

Here are "waves" you need to catch in the journey of your recovery while you are in the midst of this present crisis:

Wave #1 -- *Take care of you... First.* I know. It sounds so... wrong. And selfish. Hear me out, though... If you don't take care of yourself, you will be in no condition to take care of your family. More than likely, the situation you are experiencing is not going to be over today. Or tomorrow. Or the next day. In most cases, this is something you will have to deal with over the long haul.

If that is the case, you cannot attend to something of that magnitude without taking care of yourself. Yes, your family needs you. Yes, the injured needs you. Yes, there are realities and pressures and things flying your way. None of that gets dealt with properly if you drain yourself dry and have nothing left to give. Preparing yourself for the long haul – taking care of you – is essential to being there for those that you love.

I realize that you may not feel like eating or sleeping or even getting your daily intake of something as simple as water. If you are in the hospital right now, you may even fear walking away from the injured, lest something happen to your loved one while you are gone. But, I need to tell you... you need to take breaks. Here is how to take care of yourself. Go back to the basics.

- Make sure that you take the time to eat – especially healthy food.
- Drink water.
- Exercise… even if you are at the hospital. Walk up and down the hallways.
- Take vitamins and other supplements that support your diet.
- Sleep 7-9 hours a night (if this is next to impossible, consult your physician for sleep aides).
- Delegate the things you can (i.e. cleaning the house, taking "shifts" for the injured, etc.).
- Attend a support group.
- Don't watch the news (or other things that highlight the "negative" in life).
- Take quiet times… meditation, prayer, etc.
- Get a weekly massage.
- Go out with a friend or on a date with your spouse.
- Stay involved with your hobbies.
- Get counseling.
- Read books or articles that offer help or support.
- Take a long, relaxing bath.
- Take the time for special "treats" for yourself – chocolate, cup of coffee, etc.

You need to do the things that allow you to be a good caregiver to the ones you love. If you drain you, how will those who need the best of you get it when they most need it?

If you are at home, you need to do things that "re-fuel" you. Maybe that's a walk in the morning. Maybe it is reading. Or a cup of coffee. Or a chat with a buddy about last night's game. Whatever "it" is, you need to do that which puts energy back into you. I often hear people say that they don't deserve to do those things because their child, spouse or loved one doesn't get to do those things due to the tragedy. I understand that your heart is in the right place. But, you are believing a myth if you punish yourself hoping that, by doing so, it will make the injured feel better. On the contrary, it makes them feel worse – as if they have ruined your life, too. Depriving yourself of "re-fueling" exercises does not make the injured feel better. All they want is you. And they want the best of you. You cannot give them the best of you if you have drained your tank to the point of empty. At some point, the tank runs dry and there is nothing left to give.

Wave #2 -- You are not a victim... On the contrary, you are a survivor. So is your family. One of the biggest pitfalls for people is that they fall into a victim mentality. For this reason, I don't even like using the word "victim" when it comes to tragedy – it sets up people to think of themselves that way. When we fall prey to believing that we are mere victims, we lose whatever power we had left in reclaiming our lives. Trauma wins. However, when we see ourselves as survivors, a renewed sense of hope beckons and we start setting ourselves up for the next important wave in our recovery. You have control over how this will affect you.

Wave #3 -- What you think really does matter... Never underestimate the power of your mind. Too often, things turn out the exact way we expected they would turn out. Meaning, if we expect horrible things, that is exactly what we will get. On the contrary, expecting positive things creates space for positive things to happen. We all too often get that for which we were looking.

Think about what you want. I encourage you to do whatever you need to do to keep the negative thoughts out. They drain you, they discourage you and they train your mind to believe that something bad is around the corner. And here's the worst part about negative thoughts: they keep you stuck in fear. Just because someone told you something does not mean you have to believe it. My sister is living proof. She had to be resuscitated three times. The doctors said she would have brain damage and that she wouldn't finish high school. Not only did she finish high school, but she did so with her class – on time! She's a college graduate, business woman, wonderful mother and a beautiful person inside and out...

Anything is possible, even in the midst of the worst situations.

Wave #4 -- Be your own advocate... Put simply, if you feel something, speak up. You have choices! You have a voice! Use it. If you feel something isn't right, say so. Don't wait. Don't worry about being "nice" so as not to offend anyone. Please hear me... I am not telling you to operate outside of your comfort zone. Some people are wired in such a way that it makes it easier for them to engage friends, family, doctors, hospitals, insurance, work, church and the like in potential conflict. Others don't feel as equipped to deal with that. Either way, a strategy needs to be implemented by you and yours to advocate for that which you need in this present situation. It's up to you to set the boundaries and address that which will best help you and your family toward recovery.

Being an advocate for yourself and your family is huge. It helps in the healing process and gives you the peace of mind that you are regaining some control. Plus, it gives you power again to feel like you can make a difference. Let me give you an example. One day, my Mom noticed that my sister was struggling. She knew in her gut that something wasn't right. When she notified the nurse, she got the "brush off" and was told she was over-reacting. (A point of emphasis here: Mothers have powerful intuitions when it comes to their kids. A Mom always needs to trust her maternal instinct. Just like Dads need to trust that "gut feeling" they have.). My Mom stayed persistent and went to another nurse until she finally found someone who would listen. Sure enough, my sister's lungs were filling up with fluid. If my mother had not been persistent and had not been the advocate in that situation, my sister could have died.

I am afraid this is something you will face over and over as you go through this experience. I counsel people all the time who confuse being an advocate for themselves with the idea of being mean or rude. And, too often, that is an excuse to avoid taking responsibility for being your own advocate. There is absolutely nothing wrong with you being firm and assertive when you feel something strongly about your current situation. You don't have to take "no" for an answer. I want to give you the freedom – and right – to stand up for you and yours.

Wave #5 -- Be honest... Be real honest.... Part of dealing with what you are going through is being honest enough to admit what is really going on – inside of you, outside of you, around you, etc. All the time I hear people in my office who want to talk about the "right" way to handle things. In so doing, they prevent themselves from being truly angry, or scared, or sad, or fearful. When I ask what the "right" way is to handle things, the answer is almost always one that makes a person look controlled and appropriate to others.

When that happens, what others think has become more important than what we are going through in the situation. That isn't right – at all. We are now more concerned with taking care of others' perceptions and opinions than we are of our own reality. If you think about those you love who have been deeply affected – versus those we might be trying to impress by doing things the "right" way, who matters most to you? And what about you?

Remember, there is no "right" way to handle things, anyway. That's a myth. Everyone reacts differently and processes differently. Every situation is different. Being honest with yourself is more important than doing things the "right" way.

Wave #6 -- Let others help... It is not a sign of weakness to let other people help you with things. No one is expecting you to be Superman or Superwoman through this. And here's the thing: most people feel so helpless about your situation that being able to do anything that helps you makes them feel like they are *doing something* in your time of need.

Let me go one step further... It is okay to tell people exactly what you need. Do not expect them to just know. They really don't know what you need and really don't mind you telling them exactly. While you may not want to be a burden or you may not want to ask too much, remember... they want to help. It's why they asked. It gives them a feeling of power back, too, in the midst of this crisis.

Wave #7 – Create a blog... Another suggestion I have is to create a blog (or have a friend or family member do it for you). If you feel that people need to hear from you, then instead of making it a habit to call every single person, put the word out that you will update everyone through your on-line blog. You can post once a day (or whatever you feel up to or tell your friend to post on your behalf) and allow folks to comment back. That way, they feel connected to you and are getting the information, while you don't need to keep track of every single phone call and worry about hurting someone's feelings because you didn't get back to them. Trust me... DO NOT THINK that you can take all the phone calls. Absolutely not. They will drain you. Use the available technology to work for you and make your life easier.

Wave #8 -- Protect yourself.... I am sure this sounds strange on some level. What I mean is this: when you are in the midst of dealing with your worst nightmare, it's possible there might be people in your life who are making it worse. Perhaps a family member or friend and anyone who has that unique ability to absolutely drain your energy, irritate you and make everything worse. Way worse. I want to give you permission to stay away from these people. Screen their calls. Don't answer the door when they show up. Walk away. Route them through someone else.

A strategy that is effective is to appoint a "spokesperson" for the family – someone you trust to deal with "everyone else" and who can speak on your behalf. You can route phone calls through the spokesperson, requests from friends and family, and the constant questions and demands of you from others. The key is to make sure the spokesperson is someone who listens to you and is able to stand up for what you need. This can be a family member or trusted friend.

You only have so much fuel in your "tank." Who would you rather spend it on – the person who drives you crazy or your child or spouse? I know it sounds silly, but I often must give clients in my office *permission* to shut someone out because they feel like it is rude or selfish. I am here to give you all the permission you need. Look... you are trying to survive right now. It isn't your job to attend to that person's need who is draining you of all the "good stuff" you have to offer. That's about them – and they can find other people or areas to get that need met. Right now, this is about what you need and those close to you who are navigating some rough waters. Be intentional about who you choose to give "you" to in these days...

Wave #9 – Guard Against What Others Might Say and Think... I'm guessing that you might be thinking, "What will people think?" That is, how are people going to judge you when they see that you are taking care of yourself? After all, people love to create drama – especially when you go against what they think you ought to be doing. I have one thing to say to you about those people: forget them. They have NO IDEA what you are going through. Their attempts to judge you says everything about them and nothing about you. Your true friends and loved ones will understand completely without shame or judgment.

The others who come along – the church member who questions your motives in a prayer circle... the co-worker who wonders aloud about you at the water cooler... the relative who "would do it totally different if it had happened to her" and says as much to another relative of yours... Every week, people come to my office and explain how they are dealing with the harmful things others have said. Words are so powerful, which is why I want to caution you on which words you take into your heart and hear.

The truth is, most people don't know what to say, so they end up saying the wrong thing. People can derail you with their words – be it intentional or not. Please understand that they are naïve. By choosing to judge you rather than offer you grace, they are creating unnecessary pain for you and others. You want no part of that and don't deserve to dwell in it yourself. Refuse to allow their judgments to deter you from what you know to be right and that which is best for you.

Now... please don't get me wrong. I believe that 95% of people are good – well-intentioned, honest, loving folks. However, even these folks are naïve at times and in their honest intention to say the right thing are often at a loss as to what to say. Consequently, they say things that harm and wound you. This doesn't make them bad, but, at the same time, their words can hurt just as much. Understand that the words being thrown your way are not so much about you as they are about the person saying them. If you can keep that thought in mind, your ability to allow hurtful words to "bounce" off of you will be much greater.

Wave #10 – Give Yourself Grace... Grace is an interesting word and I may be using it in a context that is different than how you understand it. Grace, as I mean it, is the idea of lessening the burden of expectation or performance. It is rooted in a good old-fashioned concept of not being so hard on yourself. I see people in my office all the time who are so hard on themselves! I regularly ask them, "What are you trying to accomplish by being so hard on yourself?" They often reply, "It's a way of motivating myself." I then ask the obvious question... "How is that working for you? Are you getting the results you want?" Always their answer is a resounding "NO."

Look... in case this is news to you, let me break it as gently as I can. You are not perfect. ☺ Shocking, huh? To demand such high expectations of yourself – especially during this time – is crazy. Give yourself a break. Give yourself grace. I typically see people who are set on beating themselves up mentally, emotionally, and verbally for not being everything at all times to all people. That NEVER works. Never. You will not get the results that you think you want. Please take my advice on this one... give yourself a break.

Wave #11 – See Stress Through a New Lens... First of all, stress does some interesting things to people. And make no mistake... tragedy produces more than its fair share of stress. As a result of stress, people can either be balanced or imbalanced. When people are balanced, it means that they are in a place where they can manage the stress level with which they are dealing. The stress – while present – is not overtaking their ability to reason, feel, or make decisions. They are responding, not reacting.

When people are imbalanced, the stress in their lives is overtaking their ability to maintain some level of equilibrium in their mental and emotional states. In essence, the stress level is outside their ability to handle it. When someone says they are "stressed out" or in a state of "distress", they are basically saying how imbalanced they are within themselves. When a person is in that space, all sorts of things can happen. Their behavior may seem erratic or even irrational.

Behavior is typically an outward display of what is going on internally. If someone is behaving in a "shocking" way, it is often prudent to ask what they are feeling. Most often, fear is what you will find.

Fear creates an amazing amount of turmoil in our lives – and tragedy is a great producer of fear.

Remembering this can give you the insight you need into what is *really* going on inside another, or even yourself. The stress that results, then, can be understood in light of a deeper issue at play creating the nuances of behavior. That fear issue has a lot to do with the relational dynamics at play between people trying to recover from traumatic circumstances.

Since we as human beings were designed to be in relationship – and fully depend on those closer relationships in times like these when tragedy has struck – you can see how the psychology of stress plays a huge role in how we interpret the action of others and ourselves. I cannot emphasize enough how important it is to understand the results of stress. Remember, focus on the relationship – not the behavior – during this time of stress. And while behavioral things may need to be addressed, keep in mind why they are occurring rather than reacting solely to the outward behavior.

A Final Thought

These waves are important to understand as you journey through this time of your life. They help give words to what you will experience in yourself and in those around you. Don't be surprised to see them play out at odd times and in odd company. We all react to stress differently, we all cope differently and we all react to tragedy differently. As such, there is no "right answer" as to how to handle things along the way. The important thing is to journey well by being true to yourself and doing the things that will take care of you in the meantime.

At the end of the day, the question is pretty simple:

How will you take care of you today?

The answer to that question ultimately decides what kind of waves you are going to choose.

Taking care of you is a "good" wave.

It's the right wave.

And it is a wave you MUST catch during this time.

I see too many people who revert back to taking care of everyone and everything instead of themselves during times of trial. They may have had the intention of taking care of their own needs, but they too easily and quickly allow the demands of others to dominate their decision-making on what is most important.

That is not a wise move.

Taking care of YOU is of utmost importance.

Taking care of YOU is a very smart thing to do.

Taking care of YOU is the right decision.

Taking care of YOU leads to better waves along the way.

Taking care of YOU leads to a better life story.

The decision is in front of you... You can revert to tsunami-type waves that continue to wreak havoc and chaos into your world. Or, find new meaning in gently rolling sit-on-the-beach-and-enjoy waves that lead to a life of peace and transformation even in the midst of your tragedy.

The choice is yours.

CHAPTER FIVE

Finding Your Way With The Injured

First off, a reminder of the definition I laid out in the "Author's Notes" as it relates to the idea of the "injured." When I use the word "injured" I mean the person or people in your family who have physically been hurt by the tragedy... a broken body of some sort.... an illness that has been diagnosed... a disease that has been identified... a violent assault on the body that has taken place... Whatever the case, when I use the word "injured", I mean to encompass the multitude of ways a person can be hurt physically in a tragedy. Please keep that in mind as you read through this chapter.

I mentioned in Chapter One that my family had been through a pretty tough tragedy with "The Fire." In that situation, I was not the injured – my older sister was. I had the role of the "non-injured sibling." The way I experienced "The Fire" and the way she experienced it as the 'injured' were very different. While we may have shared some similar feelings and thoughts from the incident, we both walked away with very different issues with which to deal and with which to come to terms. To put it simply, I really didn't know what it was like to be the injured. I couldn't relate.

That is, until June 11, 1990.

My understanding of trauma took on a whole new meaning at the age of nineteen. I had just finished my Freshman year of college and had spent the day celebrating my older sister's graduation from college (things do get restored!). My boyfriend and I loaded up his pick-up truck and caravanned with some friends on the long road trip from Nampa, Idaho, to Eugene, Oregon. We got a late start and were going to have to do some traveling at night.

Just outside of Bend, Oregon, I had fallen asleep in the passenger side of my boyfriend's Toyota truck. A few minutes later, I awoke in a state of instant adrenaline... the truck was careening out of control.

My boyfriend had apparently fallen asleep at the wheel and awoke just in time to see us veering toward a telephone pole at 65 mph. He jerked the wheel - instantly waking me up – and the truck flipped onto its side and began to roll. Somewhere in the midst of that roll, I broke my neck. Then, at some point in the melee, I was ejected from the truck through the windshield. My kneecap was the last thing to hit the pavement, shattering it in two. Somehow the truck managed to miss me lying there on that stretch of Highway 20, fifteen miles outside of Bend.

My boyfriend was panic-stricken. Our friends in the car ahead who had seen our headlights swerve, turned around, thinking we had a flat tire. I remember being in a state of consciousness, but seemingly outside of my body at the same time. The way I landed had me lying across the highway. If another car were to come along, it would have run me over.

Knowing he had to get me out of the road, my boyfriend put his hands in my armpits, cradled my head in his forearms and dragged me to the side of the road. I found out later that such a move was the only possible way to move a person with a broken neck without possibly permanently paralyzing her on the spot.

I remember thinking how gross it was that he had his hands in my armpits! With no phone and out in the middle of nowhere, everyone decided it would be best to lift me in the back of our friend's car and drive me into Bend to the hospital. Thankfully, right then – out of nowhere it seemed – a car pulled up and a man jumped out yelling, "Don't move her!" He left his wife with us and drove the 20 miles back into Bend to get help. An ambulance came rushing to the scene, which got there just in time as the pain was starting to cascade through my body with unbelievable force.

Without going through every inch of detail, I spent the better part of the next month in the hospital. The first week was spent in traction with a fifteen-pound weight hanging off the end of my bed to hold my neck in place. I then had surgery a week later on my neck. It turned out that my C3 and C4 vertebrae were fractured and my C3 was resting on my spinal cord and had to be fused together.

Thankfully, my spinal cord had not severed. It had been nicked, causing paralysis in my left arm and leg. I remember lying in bed with that 15-lb weight hanging from my neck like it was yesterday... Oh, how painful it was whenever someone accidentally bumped my bed! I can remember vividly that week and the thoughts that raced through my mind. "Will I walk again?" "Will I be in a wheelchair for the rest of my life?" I knew so much was riding on this one neck surgery – as if my whole life hung in the balance on its outcome.

My kneecap was wired back together through an intricate surgery, the scrapes and scars tended to, and the next several weeks of my life were spent relearning how to do "normal" physical movements and independently function again. I had to learn how to walk, button a shirt, tie my shoes and all of the other things that we typically do without even thinking (To this day, it is only by sheer determination that I don't walk with a limp. Yet, every day, I continue to live in pain as a result of the car accident).

Over time, I began to get feeling and movement back in the left side of my body after the surgery. It was such a slow process. As a collegiate volleyball player, I was used to being in great shape. You can imagine how much of a dejection it was for me when I first realized that I couldn't even muster up enough strength to throw a beach ball to my toes on my first day of rehabilitation.

As the "injured," I was coming to grips with a whole new understanding of tragedy from the other side of the equation. Why had this happened to me? It wasn't even my "fault." The pain was tremendous...re-learning how to do basic tasks that I had taken for granted was psychologically and physically taxing. It would be a year until I was able to play volleyball again, and by the time I came back, I was nowhere near the player I had been. Dreams that I had of one day playing professionally were shattered.

People started to treat me differently, as if I were some sort of helpless person who needed constant assistance. And while I did need help on some things, I wanted to do things myself and not be treated as some sort of invalid who was incapable of things. I was fighting with myself over the life I wanted and the life I now had. I was hurt, angry, confused, sad, bitter, broken, ashamed, embarrassed, and shocked. To top it off, I felt ugly... my scars made me feel less attractive – and the mammoth neck brace I had to wear didn't help. I was trying to manage my own fears and anxieties and but also wishing that life could just be the way it had been once again.

As an aside, my parents were amazing during this time. They never once made me or my boyfriend at the time feel guilty. Without a doubt, my accident was torture on them, both mentally and financially. And yet, they never once put that burden on me. They were great during that time, even though I am sure that they couldn't believe that another tragedy had hit our family.

However, I still struggled with the idea that my life wasn't to be the same anymore. My dreams, expectations and how I saw myself all had to change.

I had to find my "new normal."

Stepping Into the Injureds' Shoes

When the unthinkable takes place, there is a unique set of feelings, thoughts, and ideas for the injured. It's different than what everyone else experiences and can cause damage if not addressed in a healthy way. I want to help explain to you what it is like to be in the injureds' shoes, so you can relate as best as possible to what they are experiencing. Here are the "waves" in their trauma tsunami...

Wave #1 -- The injured are likely to... re-experience the tragedy... It is very normal for the injured to re-experience what they have been through. In fact, it is highly likely that the injured will re-visit the event like it is happening all over again. They can have nightmares that make them afraid to go to sleep. Re-visiting the trauma can happen emotionally and mentally – even physically – and is something you should expect as a possibility. It's okay. And normal.

Understand, however, that this will be incredibly upsetting to the injured. Strong feelings of angst, fear, rage, sadness and the like can be involved, and you should be prepared for what you might experience as the one caring for the injured when this occurs. It will trigger strong feelings in you; you don't want the injured to hurt. Be very aware of what you are feeling.

The biggest key is to validate what they are feeling. The worst thing you can do is try to deny, shut off, or neglect the powerful feelings that exude from them when this occurs. If you attempt to derail their process – perhaps because of your own need for the pain to go away – you will actually contribute to them staying stuck in their pain and misery. The injured need safe havens to experience these feelings. You can help provide that safe haven. Please understand that their intense feelings and powerful re-living of the event is normal – what they need is someone strong enough to exist "in it" with them when the intense feelings of the trauma occur all over again.

After I had my accident, the first time I tried to sit up I passed out. Although I was probably only "out" for a few seconds, I re-lived every moment of the accident. Literally, I was there in my mind...in the truck, being ejected through the windshield, lying on the pavement... When I "came to" I was terrified. I was frightened beyond belief. I didn't know where I was or what was happening. Here's the strange thing: my body felt the exact same pain it did when I was lying out on the road.

When re-experiencing the event, the injureds' mind and body are actively trying to cope with the event itself. It is the mind and body's attempt to struggle with what has taken place so that potential danger, fear, and pain can be avoided. When the injured re-experience the tragedy, it is highly likely that they will feel like they are in danger again. Such a feeling is both frightening and out of control because they can't get it to stop. As the caregiver, it is important to "exist" with the injured in those moments (just be there) – *without trying to fix it.*

Wave #2 -- The injured are likely to... have an on-going need to process what has taken place... The injured are often attempting to reconcile what has happened so that they can bring their world-view back into equilibrium at some point. The injured are especially cognizant of this fact, as they often possess a deep need to process what has taken place in their lives. Depending on how severe the tragedy was – or the length of stay in a hospital and such – their ability to process will be much slower. It is possible that what has happened has escalated the need for heavy medication or other medical procedures which would easily delay the injureds' ability to fully comprehend and think through what has occurred. *As such, it is important to provide them a safe place in which to process – whenever they feel the need.*

Remember... this is their timeline, not yours. If you are feeling the need for them to get past what has happened, that is about you and not them. Often, this is a way for you to protect yourself from having to feel the pain that you desperately don't want to feel again. This is very difficult at times, as you struggle to "move on" in life. You must find a place to safely process your feelings – apart from the injured. Too often, that can result in wayward feelings of frustration, shame or anger as the injured is not always as far along the journey as you may be.

For example, when a client of mine arrived home after several months in the hospital, she was ready to start dealing with her injuries and the other consequences that took place as a result of her trauma. The problem was, the rest of the family did not want to go through that again. It was too painful. The family wanted her to be where they already were – or thought they were – so that *they* could feel better about *their* pain. Consequently, the message she received was to "bury it" which made her more angry and set back her efforts to deal with the real life consequences of the event.

The truth is the family, hadn't really dealt with it. Her bringing up things just escalated their shame over the incident – so much so that all they wanted to do was avoid the subject altogether. As a family, all they ended up doing was creating a vicious cycle that led to more unhealthy habits of dealing with the tragedy. They pretended things were okay when really they were not.

Wave #3 -- The injured are likely to... be very angry. If you think about it, they have a right to be. They need to be! Imagine all of the pain they have (and not just physically). Dreams have died. Life is different. How they perceive themselves has changed. How people treat them has changed.

They may have lingering physical issues. They may start thinking and be concerned with issues that they never considered prior to that moment (i.e. "Will I be able to have children?" "Does insurance cover me in the future?" "Will I go into remission or is this it?" etc.)

My car accident occurred 21 years ago and I feel pain in my body every day. There are times when I am angry about it – 21 years later!!

The injured need to be given permission to be angry. Short-circuiting the process of being angry dramatically hinders the process of healing and coming to grips with reality over time. The truth is, if you let them be angry, the anger will not last as long. People's fear often is that, if you let someone be angry, they will stay angry. Nothing is further from the truth. Letting people express their anger helps get them past it. Anger unexpressed leads to depression. Anger expressed can become a pathway to healing.

As the parent or caregiver, it is important to remember that "anger" is what therapists or psychologists define as a "secondary emotion." Meaning, it is always an expression of something that is primary or deeper. Often, that is fear, sadness, loss, hurt, or disappointment. In a therapy setting, anger is often used as a segue to get to the primary emotions. Allowing the injured to express anger can help the healing process begin quicker and with better results along the way.

Stifling anger often comes from a family system that has an inherent need to "appear" a certain way to others. The injured are forcefully or subtly told to have the "right" response so that they "don't look angry" and appear to be "handling everything just fine."

Talk about a way to derail the entire healing process! Flee from this at all costs. There is a backfire that can occur if a family feels the need to make the injured appear "fine." If anger is not allowed, at some point, it can be used as a defense mechanism to keep people at a distance. If this occurs, it is entirely possible that this mechanism will get turned on you, the parent/caregiver! You must ask yourself, "Is that what I want?"

A common inclination of families is to encourage the injured to be better than they really are. A client of mine once explained how, after a tragedy that hurt her deeply, her family wanted her to put on the "happy face" and keep smiling to give everyone the impression that "things were okay." Her family thought if you weren't angry, it meant you were trusting God. If you were angry, than it meant that you were not trusting God. And honestly, appearances to others in a church setting mattered to them at the time.

But the problem is... That doesn't work! This is not a fake-it-til-you-make-it proposition. This is real life pain and misery. There are probably some days that the injured have no desire to smile, no desire for things "to be okay." Is that alright? If you find yourself arguing "no," I would challenge you to look deeper within yourself to figure out what has been triggered for you. Why would it not be okay for the injured to have a bad day? My hunch is that, if they feel that way, it makes you feel out of control, worried and powerless. When we feel stuff we don't like, we try to force others to feel differently than they do so that we might feel better. Strange as it may seem, it is a game we play all the time... and it is a serious hindrance to healthy recovery.

Of course, we all know that certain someone in our lives who is so angry that he drives the others around him crazy. Often times, our fear is that we might create this if we let the injured embrace their anger to that extent. We don't want to encourage our family member or child in any direction that promotes *that* type of attitude and behavior over the long haul. Truth be told, letting the injured be angry will not turn them into that person you have in your head. It takes much more than that...

When it comes to anger and the injured expressing it, encourage them to let it out! Go so far as to tell them... "Tell me about your anger. I can handle it. I am here for you." There are several tangible ways for people to get their anger out:

- Give them an "anger" pillow that they can punch.
- Have them keep personal journals about the things that make them the most angry.
- Provide some magazines and have the injured cut out pictures for a collage and then give them the opportunity to cut it into pieces.
- Use a permanent marker to write angry thoughts on some rocks and then have a time when the injured can throw them into the ocean, or a lake or stream.
- Similarly, the injured can write thoughts or words that identify their anger on balloons and then let the balloons go up into the air until they vanish from sight.
- Write a letter to the one who the injured feel wronged them – a letter you never end up sending.

The key is, don't wipe away their tears as they cry... let them cry, even scream for that matter. Encourage them to get it out of their body. The more you can be a safe place for them to release the anger they feel, the better their journey past the anger will become.

Wave #4 -- The injured are likely to... feel like their lives are over. This is a tough one, because, in a sense, they are (as they knew it). The "old normal" has gone away and a "new normal" awaits. The key is when they say, "life is over." Don't argue with them. Let it be okay for them to feel that way. While we know that lives aren't "over", their belief in the dreams they once had for themselves may be.

This is especially true for those who are disfigured or have suffered some sort of permanent disability. It is SO difficult to see yourself in this new light. Truthfully, it is a HUGE loss. It is something that has to be grieved over time, so that eventually, acceptance can win out. Do not be surprised if, in the middle of feeling like life is over, they cling tightly to who they were before the tragedy ever occurred. If they do this, they will get stuck. However, as the parent/caregiver, you have to be willing to listen and gently reassure the injured into redefining themselves – without denying the power and reality of the way they feel.

This can feel like quite the tightrope act, but it is one that you are very capable of doing. When love and grace lead the way before your thoughts and actions, the power of your relationship with them will help nudge them toward a newer, healthier, and better view of themselves. This is a process – really a journey - that can take a very long time.

When the injured embrace their new lives, amazing things are going to happen. I am a counselor today because of the tragedies in my life. I get to help people heal on a daily basis – something I would not have been able to grasp if I had not gone through the things I have. I "get it" in ways I would never "get it" from a book or class.

Wave #5 -- *The injured are likely to... need permission from you to not assume their role in the family system.* Especially for children, this phrase is true. There are so many "hidden" concepts, ideas and agendas in family systems that are known to family members, but not verbally expressed. When tragedy hits, these have not gone away. They are still there. Consequently, children may still try to play the role they took on before the tragedy took place.

The injured who were the compliant children before will try to remain compliant children afterward – even if they are in tremendous physical, emotional and mental pain. "I'm okay, Mommy," they might say, even though they really aren't. The kids who were assertive and aggressive before being injured might try to return to assertiveness and aggressiveness to "impress" or show the others who expect them to be like that. "See, Dad... I'm tough," they might announce.

When forced to act as they did prior to the trauma (so the family system can be relieved of its stress), these kids are pushed into a more unhealthy state. This can cause harm to their recovery and family relationships.

Right now I want you to do something... Close your eyes and think about when you were ten years old. What was your role in your family? How about at fifteen years old? Twenty? Were you "invisible" so as not to be a burden? Were you the peacemaker who had a way of calming things down? Were you the comedian who made people laugh – especially when tension was around? Were you the over-functioning child? Perhaps, underfunctioning?

Now... as an adult, do you still play that role? We tend to keep the role we had (even go so far as to marry someone with opposite traits so we can keep our role, no matter how much we may have hated it). If this is true for you, then what is the message that the injured are dealing with right now? What are their roles? Do they still have them? Have they changed? All of this and more is at play, which is why it is so important to give them the space they need to feel the way they do.

Wave #6 – The injured need you to be okay with their true feelings. Furthermore, give your injured children or loved ones the permission to feel EXACTLY the way they do. I need to tell you one thing loud and clear: Allow your child or loved one to feel – *without it being a reflection on you as a parent.*

Just because the injured feels a certain way does not mean you have failed as a parent or spouse. I am a parent and spouse and I realize this is easier said than done. I have not handled this the best at times. Several clients I have counseled report that when they don't like the way their kids behave, they quickly move to shut them down and get them "back into line" – the role they need them to play in their family so they can feel better about themselves as parents. No parent is proud of these moments, and when they happen, the best thing to do is to go to the child and apologize.

You are wonderfully suited to help your injured loved ones feel what they need to feel. In those moments where your own "stuff" gets the best of you, take the time to go back and apologize. Perhaps the most powerful words you can ever say to your loved ones are "I am sorry." And isn't it true that we mess up as parents, spouses and loved ones on occasion? I know I do. These words mean the world in a loving relationship. Creating this dynamic in your relationship is more important than your concern in the moment about how your loved ones' feelings are being perceived by others. Give them the permission they need – and you will get the relationship that you want as well.

Your Role in the Injureds' Journey

Frankly, what I am about to tell you will probably seem confusing. My guess is that you will see this as a "balancing act" of sorts, and... you're probably right. Tragedy creates so many difficult dynamics that trying to be aware of them all can be overwhelming. I want to encourage you that, while you won't get it all perfect, you can get it "enough" that true healing, recovery and restoration can begin to take place. Your role in the injureds' "journey back" will be full of some complex moments, but use these waves as a guide to prepare yourself for what lies ahead as you help them find calmer waters in their journey back to the ocean... and embracing their "new normal":

- ***Wave #1 -- Treat them like you treat everyone else, but don't.*** Paradoxical, isn't it? The injured are aware they are "different" (whether this is true or not). As such, they may be looking for ways in which you will treat them as the frail, injured victim they suppose themselves to be. If you do, it's their way of off-loading the blame on you as to how they feel. So, don't treat them that way.

  At the same time, be aware that they may need special treatment when it comes to certain things. People with disabilities don't want to be treated as "disabled," but need you to remember that they do have some physical limitations. Does that make sense? It is a balancing act for sure, but one that you are capable of handling because of your relationship with your injured loved ones.

- ***Wave #2 -- Don't try to "make up" for what happened.*** You can't. Nothing you can do can make up for it, so don't try. If you start down that road, you will reinforce to the injured that they are "victims." A victim mentality never helps get someone back on the path of recovery. We have all seen what happens when people embrace being victims – they begin to feel a sense of entitlement. (i.e. "this happened to me so I deserve this").

Be careful not to refer to them as victims. Instead, treat them as "survivors." This will keep them from falling into the entitlement trap. The entitlement idea, once it gets rolling, can certainly play upon any guilt you feel. The message the injured need is, while bad things have happened, there are great things ahead. They need to know that they can "fly"... that you believe in them and their ability for greatness.

- *Wave #3 -- Do not allow false guilt to get the best of you.* This goes along with trying to "make up" for what happened. I have seen families and parents who have bought things for the injured child that they would never buy for their other kids. If you would not have bought it for the injured before the tragedy, don't buy it now.

Sometimes, families require less of the injured, expect less of them, and refuse to hold them responsible for basic elements of their lives. Think about how this sets them up for the rest of life!

When it comes to injured children, I have seen families who have come up with two different sets of "rules" for the kids: one for the injured and one for the non-injured. Think about the discord that is going to create in your family, should you choose to do that – not to mention the self-perception that the injured will take on in the months and years to come.

- *Wave #4 -- Do not do for the injured what they can do for themselves.* Oh, this is so hard! Think of it this way: when a person has young children, you often hear the line from a child, "I can do it myself!" Whether it be tying shoes or spreading the peanut butter on a sandwich, there is an empowerment that comes for the child in having done it all by himself. And while an adult knows that the end result could have taken less time (with better results) had the adult done it in the first place, the adult also knows that the future payoff in empowerment for the child is worth it.

A client of mine tells the story of coming home from the hospital and how she would try to do things herself. Her Mom would stop her and say, "No, you can't do that" and make her other siblings attend to whatever it was. It made her siblings resent her and her Mom. Without question, her mom's heart was right – she wanted to help – but the methodology was wrong. When stuff like this happens, the message to the injured is, "You are incapable. You are disabled. You are not strong enough." The other message that gets sent to the injured is that they can make mom or dad or spouse feel guilty enough to get whatever they want.

When tragedy strikes, it is natural for the injured to regress. It is normal for parents of injured children to see the "little boy or little girl" come out in them again and it makes them feel good to be able to care for them at that "stage" again. While you never want to make a person feel badly for the regression – it is normal and can happen to adults as well – you don't want to encourage or enable them to stay in the regressed place. If you take care of what they could take care of themselves, you will help them stay stuck rather than helping them journey toward life again. And don't worry about the regression... they won't stay there – but don't help them stay there, either...

- ***Wave #5 – Stay balanced.*** Remember when I told you that the first thing you have to take care of in all of this is YOU? This is why. Injured loved ones need you to stay balanced with your stress through all of their moments and cycles of imbalance. This is not to say that you won't still have your moments. The truth is, you will. But, as you may have noticed, the task is exhausting. However, they need you in a good place so that they can lean on your relationship.

  The ability to develop a relationship with the injured is dependent on the way you manage your stress and stay balanced. Without experiencing a balanced feeling from an adult, a child cannot connect in relationship to a parent figure. Spouses and loved ones cannot, either. Balance breeds safety, which breeds connection. In trauma, connection is HUGE. Your injured loved ones need your ability to balance yourself even more than they did before.

- ***Wave #6 -- Prepare the injureds' world for their arrival.*** What I mean is, help the others who are a part of the injureds' lives to understand the reality of their situation now and what they can expect once the injured re-enters the fold. For example, my sister now visits schools on behalf of kids who are burn survivors, helping their classmates understand what has happened and how to relate back to the injured. She lets the kids touch her skin and scars and relates to them in a way that helps them relate to their injured classmate. This is a great concept, especially when disability or disfigurement has occurred. Paving the way for others to re-enter your loved ones' lives helps them journey back to "life" in some very powerful ways.

- *Wave #7 -- Don't act like nothing ever happened.* That is simply denying reality. At the same time, don't go too far the other way in always making it the focus so the injured stay injured. This is a daily task that you should prepare to deal with over the long haul. It is okay to talk about the story of what happened. In fact, letting everyone contribute what they remember can often be very healing. In the context of loving relationships, this type of interaction is not re-traumatizing. Quite the contrary, it is a way of mastering the story which can go a long ways toward healing.

- *Wave #8 -- Ask for help.* This is very hard to hear, but... often times, our kids or spouse who have been hurt or are ill will respond better to someone else. If you are constantly struggling with helping the injured get dressed or dressing their wounds (or whatever else), do not think for one second that you have "failed." Let someone else help. Set up yourself and the injured for success by removing the obstacles that keep you in conflict. If that means having someone else help them with whatever is needed, then do it!

Allow others to help you so that the relationship you maintain with the injured is the best it can be. There are many resources now. Talk to the social worker or nurses at the hospital since they often have a great list of local resources. An internet search can produce many services in your area, including in-home care. You do not have to be the sole caregiver. It is not worth being in constant conflict.

- **Wave #9 -- Listen.** Injured loved ones are going to grieve. And grieve. And grieve. This is going to take time and it will come and go at some of the most unexpected moments. It's okay. Your job is to become a great listener to what they need. Listening is just that – listening. Often times, you don't even need to say anything. You just need to be there. Respect what they say, respect what they need, respect how they feel.

 We talked about how to relate to anger. It's worth saying again: when the injured feel angry and you don't know what to do, do this... just listen. They'll be better off. *You'll* be better off. The worst thing you can do is to tell the injured, "You shouldn't feel that way." If you are tempted to do this, remember... it is more about your pain than theirs.

 We think internally, "If they would just stop feeling _____ (fill in the blank), then I wouldn't have to feel _____ (fill in the blank)." The injured need you to be okay with whatever they feel. They need to know that you can handle it. Again, staying balanced in your stress is key, keeping in mind the bigger picture is your goal.

Arriving Home

I don't know the particular tragedy you and yours have been through, but I do know that if it has involved any time away from home at all (i.e. hospital, treatment center, rehabilitation center, etc.), coming home changes life radically. All too often, we really aren't prepared for the day the injured arrive home. The reason? We can't wait for their arrival home so life can get back to "normal." But remember… life needs to take on a "new normal" now!

There are other things that typically we are not prepared for when the injured come home. For example, a hospital provides structure and safety – there are people there who are trained and knowledgable about the particulars of the care needed for the injured. While "going home" sounds wonderful, there is also an element of fear related because we really aren't totally sure how all of this is going to work. Now, instead of someone who is "always there" in a hospital setting, it is just you and yours. Sadly, many friends and extended family members often think the situation is over because you are now out of the hospital and at home. Consequently, they stop offering help because they (incorrectly) think that things are back to normal.

There will be the constant desire and temptation among your family to want things back the way they *were*, not what they *are* now. This is dangerous. While we all understand what is meant, that thinking leads to a dangerous path. **The truth is, you can't go back.**

And here's the thing: that doesn't have to be bad!!

It is possible that the life you are about to engage is even better than the one you had previously! It can be a great thing. As I look back on my own story and that of my sister, I would never want to relive those incidents. The pain was tremendous. The heartache piercing. I never thought that anything good would come out of it.

But you know what? Here I am, many years later. My relationship with my older sister after "The Fire" has turned into one of the greatest friendships of my life. I went from having to re-learn how to walk to running the Los Angeles Marathon. I am a counselor today because of my experiences and get the privilege of helping others. I am even writing this book because of the joy I have experienced on the "other side" of tragedy.

And you know what? This can be you, too.

This can be your injured loved ones, if they choose.

CHAPTER SIX

Finding Your Way With Non Injured Children

Remember the oxygen mask? As a parent, you put on your oxygen mask first before assisting your child. Those are the flight attendant's instructions. If you ever needed your mask first, it is because of what I am about to tell you.

I completely understand that your focus right now is on the injured in your family, be it a child or spouse. How could it not be? As important as that is, I want to caution you on something.

Do not overlook the non-injured children in your home.

When "The Fire" happened in my family, my sister Jamie and I took on new roles in our family. I became the over-functioning, thirteen-year-old miniature adult who was attempting to fill the "mom" role while my mother was attending to my sister, Kim, in the hospital. I did it all around the house – as my mother had done previously – and won accolades from family and friends alike for being so "helpful" and "responsible." My sister, Jamie, rebelled. She adopted the attitude that she would do as she pleased and played out that role by breaking rules and bending boundaries at home. She didn't win accolades... she received negative reactions from Mom and Dad.

Here's the thing: we were both after the same thing but tried different avenues to get it. "The Fire" had affected us, too, except we had no physical scars to prove it. We weren't the ones "hurt." But, we were both hurting. In the craziness of our family tragedy, we both were fighting against being "overlooked." The only way to compete with our injured sister was to create roles for ourselves that garnered us attention in hopes that someone might attend to the pain, guilt and anger we felt inside.

Our story is not dissimilar to hundreds of other clients I have seen through the years. When it comes to tragedy, most of the counseling in my office has been the result of the "other" children in the home feeling lost or overlooked when the family tragedy occurred. In many cases, we are talking about grown adults coming to see me after years of dealing with what happened to them as kids after the family tragedy took place. And, almost always, the story is the same: **they weren't hurt, but they were deeply hurting.**

I have read literally hundreds of pages of material on dealing with kids and parents who have been struck with tragedy and how to treat and mentor them through their injuries as the "injured." There is considerably less amounts of material on what it is like to be the "non-injured" one. We expect the non-injured to move on in life, going back to the activities and pursuits they had before the tragedy took place. After all, it's not like the whole thing happened to them.

Except… it did.

I cannot stress enough just how crucial it is as a parent to understand this side of the equation – for reasons I will explain in this chapter. I am passionate about this because of having lived it myself and seeing it so often with my clients. If the other children in the family are overlooked, it can extend the effects of the tragedy or even cause secondary trauma.

Here is what I mean by that: the dynamics of parenting are significantly altered by tragedy. When the event happens, you are overloaded with what is urgent. Most of the urgency involves the injured. This is a break from the norm of your parenting style, that's for sure. Your other children sense this. And, they probably understand. However, as the urgency continues to drag on (based on the extent of the injuries or illness), it is entirely possible that a whole new pattern of parenting has emerged that is different from what the other children in your family need. The non-injured children then, attempt to draft new roles for themselves to fit into the new pattern that has been created. They may do this for a variety of reasons, such as:

- **_The "hero" reaction_**. They see you, the parent, attempting to be the "hero" to their injured sibling. You are there attending to every need, and they want to somehow contribute as well. As with you, it may feel to them like they have regained control or power by doing so. They "rally to the cause," denying their own needs in order to fit in with the family paradigm of attending to the injured. Just like you, their own needs do not go away, and they end up with a conflicted sense of what to do.
- **_The competition reaction._** Over time, the non-injured may feel (whether true or not) that they cannot "compete" with the

injured. The competition is for attention – primarily from parents – so that they can feel accepted, cared for and loved. Children do not understand the depth of all that is going on in trauma and therefore cannot approach it in the same way as adults. It is not as easy for them to set aside what might seem like selfish needs.

- **_The sacrifice reaction._** Children, while not understanding the depth of tragedy, do get that certain things have to happen in order for life to function in the family. They perceive needs that the injured have and, more significantly, perceive the needs that you have and try to fill those needs themselves. In so doing, they "reverse" the parent/child relationship and attempt to take care of you.

- **_The guilt reaction._** In much the same way as you have probably felt, non-injured children may feel guilt for what has happened. They may even honestly believe it was their fault. They struggle with guilt and, because they are children, don't know how to process it in a healthy way.

They are likely to have "survivor's guilt" (i.e "Why didn't it happen to me?"). "Survivor's guilt" is a difficult struggle, especially for a child. They feel guilty they weren't the one who was hurt and at the same time, really glad they weren't. It leaves kids and adults alike in a tough spot trying to make sense of their feelings and beliefs. As a thirteen-year-old sitting by my sister's bed after she was burned, all I could think about was, "Why wasn't it me?" I hadn't been critically burned. Why not? "It should have been me," I would tell myself over and over. I was the one who ran into the house to get my sister. "She would never be in this place if it weren't for me," I kept thinking. I felt guilty. I felt responsible. I felt... lucky. And I felt wrong for feeling that way...

The non-injured may also feel guilt for requiring anything of you as a parent in their lives. They know you need to attend to the injured, but they are accustomed to you attending to their needs and don't know how to function without it. Consequently, they may attempt to do things to fill that guilt void so they can feel better inside.

- **_The anger reaction._** The non-injured may just be mad. Mad at what happened... mad that life is changing... mad that their world is different... mad that the whole thing doesn't make sense. However, it is also possible that the non-injured are mad that the tragedy interrupted their "normal" lives. It is not surprising to find the non-injured upset that the tragedy interfered with a school dance or soccer game they had. While an adult can switch gears and understand that those types of things pale in comparison to the crisis at hand, it is not as easy for a child or teenager.

I have found that these different reactions lead the non-injured children to typically adopt one of three "roles" in the family after tragedy strikes.

1) _They become "adults" – overfunctioning, very responsible and conflict-avoidant._
   This is the role I took on after "The Fire." In trying to find my "voice" or "place" in our new reality, I took on my Mom's role around the house. When Mom came back home with my sister, Kim, from the hospital, I kept my new role as an attempt to get the attention I needed. Great grades, never breaking house

rules, going above-and-beyond the expectations were all attempts on my part to react to the tragedy that had occurred.

All too often, kids bypass being a kid in order to become that miniature adult so they can have a place in the new family system. I typically can spot these kids right away when they come to my office. They seem so mature for someone 12, 13, 14, 15 years old. Unusually mature…

2) *They become rebellious, seeking to break the rules in an attempt to express their anger and dislike of the situation.* The signs of this role are clear when the child expresses feelings and thoughts of "I don't care." Nothing could be further from the truth, but they play out that attitude in an attempt to get the attention they need. They may not even be "rebellious types" but feel that such behaviors will land them a spot in the new family reality.

And frankly, it works. When kids act out this role, they get attention – *even if it is negative.* It is still attention. My sister, Jamie, would tell you the she honestly never consciously made the decision to rebel. She was eleven years old at the time and had no idea how to deal with her feelings of hurt, anger and loss. The competition reaction has a lot to do with this role, as the non-injured believe they can never "win" head-to-head with the injured for parental love. And so, they create a new life for themselves based on the opposite of what the family intended, in order to establish an identity apart from the injured.

3) *They disappear – becoming "invisible" if you will, disconnecting and doing their own thing so as to withdraw altogether from the family system.* Kids often do this as a way of taking care of the parents. One of my clients talks about becoming "invisible" in her family after a severe tragedy to one of her siblings, because it was her way of giving her parents a "gift." If they never had to worry or bother with her, they could give all of their attention to her injured sibling.

By disconnecting from the family, the non-injured also disconnect from life in some pretty profound ways. They struggle to dream, to create and to blaze their own paths... because they have chosen non-existence. I see this too often with adults who, many years later, are struggling to re-engage life after having adopted this role growing up in their families.

The role that children assume depends on their personality, their birth order and the way their parents respond to them. If you had a tragedy as a child, I would ask you... how did you respond? Can you identify with one of the three responses above?

Herein lies **_Parenting Key #1_** in all of this: **Don't assume that the way your children are behaving is what they truly want.** They may be over-functioning" because it makes them feel better. They may be disappearing because they *thought* it would be best. The non-injured children may maintain a certain way of being for long stretches – even years – as a REACTION to what they are feeling from the tragedy. But these reactions are not well thought out plans to meet the real needs and desires of their hearts... because they are, after all, still children.

This leads to **_Parenting Key #2_: _Don't paint your children as either good or bad based on the behavior you are experiencing from them._** As in the case of my sister Jamie and me, we were both after the same result. We just took different roads to get there. However, those roads were so radically different that people placed positive and negative judgments on us.

Those judgments are what led to the secondary effects of trauma in our lives. When judgment is placed – rather than someone taking the time to find out what is really behind their behavior – children can begin to "take on" the new behavior as a whole new understanding of themselves and life. Because this new understanding was based on a REACTION to tragedy, it does not indicate who a child really is.

If that false pretense is played out over the course of years, it can become a troublesome and frustrating life pattern for the non-injured. Without a doubt, this is the biggest issue I see among clients in my office… they feel like they have to be people they are not as a result of the tragedy that hit their family.

The Overlooked Kids

The problem with overlooking these kids is the on-going issues that form from patterns of thinking and behavior that are established during this time. Kids are a whole lot smarter than we think. They get it. They have the same emotional needs we have as adults – they just struggle expressing them.

The biggest thing the non-injured child needs is someone to *listen* and someone who is willing to help draw things out of them. The danger is thinking that they are "fine" because you don't necessarily see outward behavioral changes – especially if you are neck deep in attending to the injured in the tragedy. Your "radar" for accurately seeing your non-injured children might be off some. The truth is, they are not "fine." They are going to need you every bit as much the injured does. It's just going to look different.

Before this begins to feel more and more overwhelming to you, let me give you this advice: Be as available as you can and utilize the waves I lay out for you as best you can. But, also know that this doesn't have to all be on you. Someone you trust implicitly can give to your non-injured children as well – an aunt or uncle, grandma or grandpa, or dear friend. That being said, here are some "waves" that can aid in your attention to your non-injured kids and help them find the beauty and joy of the ocean again:

Wave #1 – Be honest. Look... they're smart. They're going to figure out whatever you are not telling them at some point – and then resent the fact that YOU weren't the one to tell them. They are intuitive (generally) and they pick up on things.

If they ask you how you are doing, be honest. If not, they are going to feel conflicted and unsafe altogether. You might say, "I am having a hard day. Thanks for noticing." Such honesty goes a long way with your kids.

If you just fought with your spouse or loved one and then answer their inquiry with "we're fine" in order to protect them from worrying, you are going to make them more confused. They KNOW things aren't right. They feel it. They may not be able to express it in those terms, but they KNOW... If you aren't honest, they will begin to ask themselves whether they can trust you. And, if they don't trust you, they may resort to reactionary behavior creating long-term issues. Additionally, they will have internal conflict: "Do I believe Mom/Dad's words or what my gut is telling me?" We want kids to learn to trust their gut. That comes from having the trust in their parents validated by what Mom and Dad are saying.

Wave #2 – Understand that kids grieve differently. A kid may be fine and playing one minute and be a wreck the next. As adults, we feel things building within us. Kids tend to "flip" from one emotion to another more rapidly. Kids tend to not stay sad very long. They can go from crying to wondering if they can pull out the Legos and start building a kingdom.

They process in different ways, as well. They may ask a question in a matter-of-fact fashion that a normal adult would feel needed to be asked with some tact and compassion. It's just their way of processing because they haven't yet learned those types of social skills.

Wave #3 – Give them the facts. Kids will naturally want to know the facts surrounding the situation that has taken place. They want to know what happens next, possibilities of the future, and answers to "What If?" – just like the rest of us. Tell them the truth. This does not mean you have to give them all the details. Tell them what their age allows them to understand, but give them the courtesy of knowing the facts so that their anxiety about the unknown in their world can be eased.

Wave #4 – Listen to how they feel. Ask. Listen. Then ask again. But be prepared. Listening to your child can easily elicit feelings of guilt, anger, shame, fear and resentment in you as the parent. If you are not aware of this before you begin the conversation, you might shut them down because of your own issues in dealing with the crisis. In so doing, you might think you are minimizing their pain but what you are really doing is minimizing your own. Your children are not trying to hurt you in their honesty. They need a safe place where truth can be spoken, heard and accepted. I beg of you to never say the words, "You shouldn't feel that way." What they feel is real to them. Let that be okay. They want – and need – a voice. You can give that to them and it is one of the most incredible gifts you will ever give your child.

When they talk about their anger, refer to the tips I mentioned in the last chapter. Those ideas can help with the non-injured, too.

Wave #5 – Don't try to fix it. This is a recurring theme throughout this book. As parents, we don't want our kids to hurt. We want to protect them. Parents attempt to change the experience of the non-injured, as well, in order to fix things. That's a trap. Don't fall for it. What's done is done.

The truth is your children want you to understand what their experience has been like. If you can allow them to express all of their feelings, you will develop a wonderful relationship that really aids in the recovery from tragedy for the non-injured child. Have you ever found yourself telling your child to stop crying? Mostly, you just can't stand listening to it because of what it evokes in you. However, the most powerful thing you can do is pull them into your lap, wrap your arms around them and let them cry. You don't have to say a word – your presence as a parent is powerfully healing in that moment.

Wave #6 – Resist the "making promises" temptation. Tragedy has hit. Guaranteed, one of the questions your other children will ask is, "Is

_____ going to be okay?" Don't lie. It always backfires. If you say "yes" and the true answer is "maybe" or "no", your children will learn not to trust what you say. It's better to say "I don't know" – especially if you don't.

If you say "Yes" and the injured child or parent dies, your non-injured children will become very angry with you for the falseness of your words. They will certainly feel like you have lied. As hard as it is to feel their pain, it will help them in the long run.

Wave #7 – Stay present. Oh, this is so hard! You're exhausted, you're tired of giving, and you feel emotionally drained through it all. And yet your child needs you in this moment. Giving the non-injured valuable minutes of your time where you are fully present is an incredible gift to them. There is nothing that makes children feel more safe than the total presence of their parent. Do the best you can, remembering that others can help in this area.

Look… it is nearly impossible to be everything for all of your children during times like these. So don't be. Do your _reasonable_ best. Give yourself a break. Find someone your non-injured children can relate to so that you can have some help in attending to their needs. Giving your children your presence as you are able – and backing that up with another adult you trust who has a great relationship with your kids – is a winning combination in being there for the non-injured in your family.

If you feel like even more is required, you should consider a professional counselor for your children in this area as well. If you feel that is needed, please do not hesitate to make that call. You will be doing what smart parents do to give the best to their children.

Wave #8 – Understand that the conversation may take place over and over again. Like I mentioned earlier, this is sometimes due to the developmental stage of children. It takes them awhile to begin to understand the depth of the trauma that has occurred.

It takes longer for things to soak in with kids. You may find yourself explaining the same thing over and over. While this may feel exhausting to you, this is normal for kids – especially younger kids. The reality of life takes time with them as they seek a way to figure out their place in the "new world" that has been handed them.

However, it is also possible that something is stalling the process. Frankly, some of the questions may be ones that you don't want to ask yourself. Are you somehow stopping your children from expressing some particular feeling? Are you really able to handle their pain and anger? What happens to you inside while they are expressing their feelings?

I realize these are tough questions and put even more of a demand on you, but these are the things we signed up for when we decided to become parents. If you shut down at some point in the process, children will feel it. Having had my own children and counseled lots of kids, I am constantly amazed at their ability to perceive and understand on an intuitive level what has taken place. They just know. Honestly, if you get stuck in the process or shut down at some point, so will they. They learn from your model and example and are wonderfully adept at mirroring what they see.

Owning Things Yourself

There is no question... the job of a parent is tough. Really tough. Especially now. Your attempt to be there for your non-injured children is going to push you to the limit. But, I want you to know that, in time, your effort will not go unrewarded. When you see them excel later in life and become all of whom they were created to be – free from the guilt and shame of the tragedy – you will bask in the warmth of a grateful heart and a close and enriching relationship. There is no greater feeling than that.

That's why the toughest part of this chapter is owning this: You cannot help your child if you haven't dealt with things yourself. Go get counseling. I tell my clients who come see me for counseling that I can only take them as far as I have been willing to go myself in the therapeutic process. I have been to counseling myself – to further my own life and also so I can be someone who has "walked the walk" as well. This is something you have to be willing to do. Think about this: more than likely, you are the non-injured, too. You experienced the event. You have something in common with your non-injured children. And that something is huge... for you and for them.

Let me give you an example of this from a client of mine. "Janice" went through counseling trying to deal with the tragedy that had affected her family and her (a sibling diagnosed with a severe illness). She discovered that one of the outcomes of the tragedy was that she couldn't directly ask to get attention or be heard. That was a direct result of the trauma. She didn't have "the right" to those things because she wasn't the one who was ill.

After she was in counseling for a time, she recalled a change with her mom and dad. She was trying so hard to get their attention. Through their interactions, her mother was telling her, in essence, that she was not the "injured" so therefore didn't deserve it. So... "Janice" found a loop hole. She loved tennis. She played it all the time. Yet, she recalled she was always getting injured – her knee, her back, her ankle... What she couldn't realize at the time was that she was unconsciously figuring out a way to get her mom and dad's attention. She learned that, if she got "hurt", they would be there for her.

The problem, of course, was she was competing with someone who had an extensive illness. In order to get her due, she had to be hurt badly. A few months after her sibling's diagnosis, she encountered a very serious illness herself that put her in the hospital. In a very strange way, she was so thrilled with the illness. She was amazed at all the attention she was getting. She loved it and totally resented it.

She felt like she had to be seriously sick to get her parent's attention. While most of her attempts were much more benign than that, she knows for a fact there were times she got hurt intentionally or way over-dramatized any sports injury she encountered. But, she really had no clue as to why. When she came to realize what she had done, she was thoroughly embarrassed.

Just out of curiosity, have any of your non-injured kids recently gotten "hurt"?

Dr. Brian Johnston conducted a fascinating study at the University of Washington. He found that when a child in the family has been injured to the point of hospitalization, all the children in that family are at risk of getting hurt within the three months following the injury – usually with an entirely different injury. This phenomenon, which he calls "post-traumatic arousal," occurs when siblings are so traumatized by the original tragedy or injury that they become on the edge themselves. The siblings become jittery or perhaps worried to the point of distraction, causing them to be more likely to be injured because they are worried about being injured.[2] Isn't that fascinating?

Non-injured kids are experiencing the trauma you have been in every bit as much as you. It's why your process is so crucial to theirs. The more you progress along the lines we have discussed, the more likely you are to be in a position to unlock the feelings that they need to express in the midst of this. And here's the thing: ***you are perfectly equipped as their parent to do exactly that.*** You have unique insight into your kids that no one else has. You know them. You raised them. You have loved them through all sorts of things in this life. Consequently, you are able to give to them in a way that they need, when they need it. But, like I have said... so much depends on how you take care of you.

You CAN do this. You have what it takes.

---

[2] Perry Class, M.D., "Accident Prone Children? That's Just a Myth..." Sun Sentinel.com, June 15, 2010, September 2011, <http://articles.sun-sentinel.com/2010-06-15/news/sfl-accident-prone-myth-061510_1_center-for-injury-research-post-traumatic-stress-families>

CHAPTER SEVEN

Finding Your Way Between The Differences Of Men and Women

Let me state the obvious: men and women think differently. I am sure that this is not earth-shattering news. However... consider this: tragedy produces the opportunity for the differences in men and women to become problematical during the crisis.

You would think just the opposite. You would think that an experience like this would bring people together – especially a husband and wife who are walking through crisis together.

Sadly, that often is not the case. Tragedy can heighten the differences between men and women over time so dramatically that couples may fall into a pattern of deterioration that ultimately leads to a severe fracture in their relationship. It has been common knowledge for years that crisis can lead to divorce.

Tragedy exposes the differences in the way men and women think, react and respond. All too often the result is the break-up of a marriage that was previously a very solid relationship.

But... that doesn't have to be the case.

If you understand and respect the differences between men and women, you can actually thrive during this time.

Imagine... taking the strengths of men and the strengths of women, maximizing them to confront the road ahead.

Imagine... understanding each other's reaction to trauma so that unneeded shame and guilt would not find its way into your relationship.

Imagine... being such a great team that you can give each other grace in understanding how the tragedy affects the other and allowing that to be okay.

Imagine...

That can be you. Here's what you need to know...

Let's start with some generalizations to which you can probably relate. I'm a woman and I sometimes marvel at the mind of my husband. He can remember intricate details of a round of golf or a game of basketball he played in the 10th grade, but he has had the toughest time remembering to set out the garbage on Tuesday mornings for the last eight years. How is that possible?!?

On the other hand, my husband is flabbergasted how I can be shopping for shoes and remember that I needed to call someone back about the PTA deal at school – which relates to whether I laid something out for dinner, which in turn reminds me to text my friend about the barbeque a month from now, which in turn relates to how I feel about our social life and whether we are keeping our life in balance, which in turn relates to an issue I once had with a friend of mine, which then relates back to the shoes I was originally looking for, which seem to be at the first store we visited an hour earlier.

It's no wonder he feels like he needs to sit down and rest right there in the store.

I suppose he would take a nap, if he could. He just doesn't get it. If you are married or in a relationship with someone of the opposite sex, you get what I am talking about. Is it possible for men and women to come together in such a way as to survive – and thrive – through tragedy?

Yes.

Let me give you a few "rules" to live by in the "men and women" category so you can start this journey out right together.

1) ***Tragedy is more than likely to trigger any relationship issues you had before it occurred***. If something wasn't working beforehand, more than likely it will be exposed as a result of the crisis. Expect this. It is normal. And it is nothing of which to be ashamed – even though you may feel the embarrassment of it. Everyone has relationship issues. Accept that you are normal like everyone else.

2) ***Men and women experience and respond to tragedy differently.*** The sooner you can accept this, the better. It is a fact, pure and simple. As a side note, this could be a great thing, should you choose to view it that way. I will explain more about this later in the chapter.

3) ***You cannot change the basic ways men and women respond.*** So... don't even try. Don't fight against that which you can't change anyway. It's futile. It is a much better use of your time to understand this, anticipate it and use it to your advantage.

Keeping these things in mind, let's take a specific look at the differences between men and women and how that might affect responses to trauma.

Men

Let's start with the guys... And please keep in mind that these are generalizations in order for you to better understand the likelihood of what is going on. There is a good "room" analogy that highlights the differences in the brains of men and women. Think of a man's brain as a long hallway with rooms on either side that have doors to enter each room.

In order for a man to associate with a "subject," he must walk down the hallway and find the room that is connected to that subject. He has to open the door, enter, and then close the door so that he can focus on whatever that room represents.

The way a man's brain is wired only allows him to operate in one room at a time. So, if a man is at work (in the "work" room), he is at work and nowhere else. If he is playing a sport, that's where he is in his brain. It's the same with just about every other possible subject (room) that is out there. He can only occupy one room at a time.

Given this reality, men have the ability to be singularly focused on whatever it is that occupies the room that they are in. They are not distracted by other thoughts, concerns or ideas – those are located in other "rooms" in their brain, and they must consciously choose to walk into those rooms in order to acknowledge them. Because of this, men tend to be very good problem solvers – they can stay in one room long enough to deal with the issue present in that room.

You may have heard it said before that men "compartmentalize" most everything. In a sense, that is true. Their surroundings do not necessarily dictate which room they occupy in their brain. For example, a man could be standing in the kitchen at home but be in his work room in his head. The beauty for a man is that he is able to leave one idea in one room in his head, walk out, close the door and enter another room with something different altogether – *and the two don't necessarily have to connect.*

Interestingly enough, this can also be true for a man in the "physical" sense. He can be in one room of the house – literally – and go to another, completely leaving the old room behind. This is why a man can have an argument in the kitchen with his wife and then go to the bedroom and be interested in having sex with her, while she is still reeling from the conversation. He is in the bedroom now and the argument got left in the kitchen – both physically and mentally.

The downside is that men can have trouble multi-tasking. That is, they have difficulty switching from one subject to the next quickly or entertaining two or more subjects at once. Multi-tasking involves operating in different rooms at the same time. Men are just not wired to do that.

Hear me on this... if you are a woman who thinks this is a fable – some sort of cop-out for the man – I can confidently tell you that nothing is further from the truth. Men are definitely wired this way.

However, men can be good multi-taskers as long as they are staying in the same "room" in their heads. When they are in a "room," they have a unique ability to see everything in the room.

If you want proof, watch a live football game with a man who is a sports fanatic. When he is focused on football, he can tell you exactly what all eleven players on his team are doing on any given play. He can recite for you whether the offensive guard threw the right block and whether the tailback made the correct cut. He can examine the defense in milliseconds and let you know if the offensive formation is equipped to deal with the way the defense is lining up. More often than not, he can also tell you the statistics that back up such a play or offense, the philosophy behind it and whether he agrees with what he is seeing from the coach who designed the scheme in the first place.

He can do all of this – and let you know whether the referees and umpire made the right calls as well. The ability to see and correlate that many moving parts at once is a form of multi-tasking combined with an incredible logical-reasoning ability. Men are wonderfully able to concentrate on the subject at hand, as long as they stay grounded in one room.

When they are in a "room", they can also absolutely zero in on a singular issue. This is what makes men capable of riding a particular "wave" (as we have been discussing) for an extended period of time. They are looking for answers, the bottom line or to fix whatever is not right in the room they are in.

For example, in the "communication room," a man looks for the bottom line in communication. What is really being said? He isn't interested per se in the "story" or the "details" behind the situation, he just wants to figure out how to solve it. A husband will come home and tell his wife about a woman in his office who just had a baby. His wife will ask what she thinks are the obvious questions – "Was it a boy or girl? How much did the baby weigh? What is the baby's name? Were there any complications? What hospital?" All too often, the husband might know if it was a boy or girl and that's about it. While she can't believe he didn't get the "details," he was perfectly satisfied in knowing the bottom line: a baby was born.

"Solve it and move on" is a common theme in a man's world. The reason? It sets the "room" right again so he can have peace in that room.

And therein lies a huge key in understanding the differences between men and women: ***both want peace in their world… they just go about getting it differently***.

You may have experienced this phenomenon in conversations with men in your life. For example, a man can get in a fight with another guy in a basketball game from the competitive juices that flow. The two guys scream and shout, finally deciding who was right or settling the matter through some mutually agreed upon way (even if that is an all-out fight) and continue.

Here's the crazy part: those same two guys, after the game, can both move into another "room" in their brains and go out for pizza – together!. Amazing!! Men typically move past issues once they have been solved or resolved and are ready to tackle the next thing. It is then that they are able to leave the room that they are in, close the door and look for a new room to enter. Again, this brings peace to their world.

Now... about the rooms that men enter. They love to spend most of their time in a room in which they can succeed. If you are a man reading this, you might feel the sting of that statement a little. But, it is generally true. The reason for this is you experience self-worth, confidence and peace from toiling in the rooms in which you have found success.

This can be very frustrating to a woman who needs her man to explore a room in which he may feel inadequate. She may feel like there is something that needs to be addressed, and he may avoid it. If a man doesn't enjoy or like certain rooms, he just keeps the doors to those rooms shut in his head and avoids entering them if he can.

A woman often interprets this action that the man doesn't love her or care. That's not it. He is wired in such a way that avoiding those rooms altogether brings peace to his life. In a sense, he "locks" those rooms so they do not became a drain on his everyday existence, clouding his perception of who he is in the world around him.

After a tragedy that results in hospitalization, a man may feel completely ill at ease with emotions and therefore will struggle at the hospital. While he might feel totally confident in his work "room", the "emotion" room might be something he attempts to avoid. He may even make excuses to avoid it. Consequently, he will avoid the hospital. If someone needs to run errands, he will probably volunteer – even though the woman in his life may think that running errands should be the last thing in the world he should be doing. It is important to understand why it is happening. This is typical of men. A man will generally ignore rooms that make him feel confused or feel like a failure.

Truth be told, part of working with men in a therapy setting is helping them move into rooms in which they are ill at ease, so that they might develop skills and confidence to operate more confidently in those rooms. Over time, most men accomplish exactly that. However, it does take time. When thrust into the throes of trauma, they may not have had the time they needed to feel confident about entering certain rooms in their brains.

This then relates to the way a man communicates. A man is likely to communicate if he knows he can be successful with the communication. For example, if he believes he can have a productive conversation with his wife, he will be motivated to do so. If he doesn't believe that, he will more than likely find ways to avoid it.

When in a conversation, a man who feels the conversation is pointless and going nowhere will shut down. He will do the same if he is struggling to understand (i.e. he doesn't "get" what his wife is saying). He may even blurt out what he is thinking, like "Is there a point?" or "Where is this conversation going?"

A man is also more than likely to venture forth, "Haven't we talked about this already?" Remember… if a man has felt that you had a conversation already and he felt it was resolved, that "room" in his brain has been put right and the door is closed. When it comes up again, he might be confused as to why a subject that has been "closed" needs to be addressed again.

Men... a word here about women. When a woman brings up an issue again (i.e. something you have "closed"), for her the issue is not resolved. When something is not resolved for her, she needs to talk about it. While you believe the issue is "closed," the gift you give to your wife or female companion is being open to hearing the issue again and engaging the conversation. *The key is to listen to what the woman is saying – except you are listening for the tone of feeling, rather than getting caught up with the exact words she is saying.* By doing this, you are giving her what she needs in communication. We will explain more about this later in the chapter.

Back to men... Since men spend most of their time in rooms where they are comfortable, they most often will be successful. Because of this, they are hard-wired to the concept of success. Understanding that men are motivated by success is a key component in relating to them. This success drive is so finely tuned that it spills over into hobbies and the like. If a man finds something at which he can succeed, he will spend a lot of money and time investing in it. The reason is that such an activity makes a man feel good about himself. In those moments, he has value. He has worth. He feels like he is *somebody*. And, it doesn't matter what that something is... video games, sports, computers, building, hunting, fishing, fixing things... whatever "it" is, he will find the time to do it and the money to make it happen. It matters that much to his sense of self.

The bottom line is this: men will spend a lot of time doing things that make them feel good and will ignore or avoid the things that make them feel badly.

So you can imagine what "rooms" a man wants to occupy most of the time. My guess is – if you are a woman reading this who has a man in your life – you can already name the "rooms" where he loves spending time.

Here's the amazing thing with men, though... They actually have a "room" with nothing in it. Nothing. They can enter that room and think nothing and feel nothing. And get this... there are no words in this room. Women cannot believe this – mostly because such an idea doesn't exist in their world.

I had a client come in one day who was so amazed at what she discovered about men. She explained that, for years, she and her husband would be driving on a road trip and, after a period of silence, she would ask him what he was thinking. He would say, "Nothing." For the longest time she thought he was lying. How could you not be thinking *something*? (After all, she's a woman... she was always thinking something).

Then she had a son. Once he was a little older, she asked him the same thing. "Watcha thinkin' about?" she would ask. His response was the same... "Nothing." She couldn't believe it! Having grown up with all sisters, someone was ALWAYS thinking something.

What is interesting about this "nothing" room men have is that it is their place of refuge. When they are stressed out or anxious and they need a place to relax, they will enter that room. They may even go there if they are bored. It is a way that a man balances himself out and creates space in his life to wind down from whatever he feels is causing stress in his life. If you are a woman reading this, take note: do not take the "nothing" room to mean he doesn't care. That would be a critical mistake.

The tough part for a man is when his wife or female companion asks him the dreaded question, "What are you thinking?" and he doesn't have an answer. Because he knows she is expecting something and because he doesn't want a fight or her to suspect he is lying, a man will sometimes actually make up something. Obviously, this presents some problems if both the man and woman are not aware of what is really at play.

The toughest part with this "nothing" room for a woman is the resentment that she doesn't have it. She can be jealous – or worse... downright angry. When a woman gets angry over this she may be feeling like she is carrying the "burden" because it may appear that he doesn't care. My caution to women is this: don't jump to conclusions. Be thankful they have a "nothing" room, because that is how men can de-stress. When a man is able to enter that room, slow his brain down and de-stress, the end results are much better and more helpful. It's the way he can engage the task at hand.

Women

For women, there is not a long hallway in their brain with several "rooms" to enter and exit... for a woman, there is one large "room" where everything resides. It is almost as if everything in the ocean is at play. Everything happens in that room – *because everything is connected.* Every thought, feeling, relationship, role, job and situation is connected to every other thought, feeling, relationship, role, job and situation.

This creates a very intricate network of "webs" that connect anything and everything. The beauty of this is a woman's ability to connect feelings with thoughts and vice versa, while also "connecting the dots" in correlating situations one to another. Additionally, it is this large room that gives women the ability to multi-task over a broad range of subjects. Typically, women can handle multiple things happening at once far better than men because of their ability to move around in that large room.

Let's go back to the football game analogy. While a man can diagnose everything that is happening in that "room," a woman is more than likely to notice everything else going on in addition to the football game. She's aware of the game – maybe even aware of some of the players and what the score is – but she is also very aware of who is sitting in the stands, who is with whom, the conversation going on behind her, what someone may have worn to the game that doesn't match, the weather, if she wore the right shoes, things happening on the sidelines... all the time wondering about her to-do list at work and/or at home. She notices her surroundings and sees most everything. She is in a giant room, so to speak. Whereas the man just notices the football game, she notices the game and all that is surrounding it.

If you are a man reading this, understanding that is big. Because a woman is constantly in one large room in her brain trying to make connections, her brain never shuts off. Never. Generally, a woman does not have the ability to think about nothing like a man does. And because she doesn't have that ability, she is constantly looking to connect the dots with a brain working in overdrive to do so.

It is why shopping malls are designed for women. They can go from store to store making connections regarding outfits. They may get shoes from one place, a shirt from another, pants from another and the accessories to go with it from somewhere else. They can do this and remember their entire wardrobe in their closet at the same time, making connections to clothing articles they already have with the new ones they are purchasing. They can "see" how things can go together.

A woman will visit new shops in the mall, find both the old and new displays in stores she frequents and develop a new pattern of going through the mall seemingly at will. Generally, a man will frequent the same stores he has already been to before (i.e. stores he has "success" in) and will stick to the same patterns and routine that allow him to survive the mall experience. In essence, he sticks to the same "rooms." You often find men getting an entire "outfit" at the same store so they know that the whole thing matches and goes together. And that's only if they absolutely have to go to the mall to begin with! ☺

One other thing about the mall idea... A woman will go to the mall with something in mind she needs, but will come home with a few other things because she saw them along the way and connected that those things might add or complete other items in her closet. A man generally goes to the mall for one thing and gets that one thing, ignoring everything else and thereby not looking for other possible connections of things he might need. The only exception might be if he stops by the sporting goods or grocery store on the way home to see what else he might need to improve that which he already has...

The biggest key to understanding a woman's brain is to realize that a woman defines herself by her relationships. As such, the wiring in her brain is dedicated toward making relationships "right." That is how a woman experiences peace in her world. Her job, while important, is nowhere near as important as the connectedness in her life to the others about whom she cares.

This is different than a man. A man often defines himself by his work. A woman defines herself by her relationships. This doesn't mean that a man doesn't care about relationships, nor does it mean that a woman doesn't care about her work.

One of women's biggest needs is to connect life together. The various parts of their lives that pull them in all sorts of directions – those are the very things they want to integrate one to another for congruence. To do this, they need to "process" – that is, talk through the various things they are trying to connect.

It is through communication like this that women will connect the dots. They can bring into congruence the emotional, physical, relational, and spiritual aspects of an issue. Talking is second nature to a woman – mainly for this reason. The man who is able to "talk someone's ear off" is doing it for a very different reason. A woman is looking for connection.

This is why a husband and wife sometimes have a difficult time talking – often, the goals of their communication are totally different, so they end up missing each other. If a woman gets to talking (think: processing) and a man interjects with "solutions" because he is in his "fix-it" room, she will get visibly upset. Her way to de-stress is to talk about it; his is to fix-it.

Consequently, different objectives can lead to a miscommunication, which can lead to a fight, which leads to a great deal of stress and imbalance. The end results aren't good. A man has the potential to get overwhelmed listening to a woman – he has to jump from room to room just to follow her which can be emotionally and mentally exhausting. Ironically, a woman will feel great and relieved and think, "What a great talk!" All the while, the man is left feeling totally overwhelmed.

Because women are constantly attempting to make connections, they are very aware of disconnection. This realization causes them to spend more time attempting to mend a relationship or address something that is not right in order to make the connection again. Whereas a man will lock away things that aren't right and make him feel uncomfortable in a room somewhere in the hallway of his brain, a woman will expose the disconnection in her large room because she realizes how it affects everything else. She will then address the issue until it is brought back into alignment, allowing the reconnection she wants.

So often, this is what makes communication so difficult. A woman wants to expose any disconnect, while a man typically wants to avoid it. They both want the same thing – peace – but they go about it very differently. It is interesting that the majority of marriage counseling appointments are set by women. I believe it is for these reasons. If connections are not made, then the possibility of frustration, arguments and hurt is likely to happen again.

But, the man and woman who can understand the purpose of a particular conversation can make the differences between them work to their advantage. Think about it... if you are a President from one nation and are trying to accomplish a resolution or treaty with another President from another nation, the first thing you get versed in is how the other President thinks.

What is his culture? What does he value? What are his customs, morals, manners? You take the time to get well-versed in this so that you can understand where your contemporary is coming from. He does the same with you.

When that happens, i.e., when you understand the perspective and thought process of each other, your conversation can become very productive and lead to worthwhile results.

The same is true with a man and woman who seek to have great communication. They have different "cultures," so to speak, with different ways of thinking, different rules and different approaches. If they approach communication understanding and respecting these differences, the results can be amazing (Two heads really can be better than one.) If either ignores these basic differences, the communication is destined to fail.

__The bottom line is this: women want to be loved and men want to be respected.__

A couple who gets this plays to each others' strengths. Ironically, in a hospital setting, with the amount of chaos and confusion going on, a woman often has a better grasp of how to navigate the waters (I am generalizing, of course). A man might feel a little lost at sea because he has entered one large room (literally) with many, many things all happening at once – several of which he may not know anything about. However, once the objectives have been narrowed and defined, a man can often focus singularly on one issue and arrive at a decision or conclusion much more readily. At that point, he isn't so concerned about everything else at play – he has moved into the "outcome room."

Hence, a couple willing to play to each other's strengths (and see them as such) has a much better shot at communicating well and arriving at a place that is mutually beneficial.

Back to the subject of women... let's clear up a myth. Women do not have more emotions than men. Men have just as many emotions as women. I know... you have heard it said otherwise for years. After all, women are often labeled the "emotional" ones. The truth is, men have strong feelings, too. The difference is in the way emotions are expressed.

Culturally, men have been encouraged to *not* express their emotions. For some reason, the expression of certain emotions from men labels them as "weak." For generations, fathers have told their sons, "Don't cry." The truth is, one of the most healing things that can happen is for a man to get in touch with his feelings (something that tragedy can do very well). It's even better when a man can identify them and talk about them. While that may sound more like a woman, the reality is that the expression of emotions is a basic *human* need. When a man cannot embrace all of his emotions, two things happen. First, everything may come out as anger. Second, if a man is emotionally constipated, his wife will become over-emotional because she ends up expressing his feelings for him without realizing what she is doing.

Men have what it takes on the inside to be aware of their feelings and recognize and respond to their family's emotions. It's there. But, this is where the help of a woman is so important. She is able to exist in the ocean of emotions better than a man – typically. Being able to assist in giving freedom to the man for expression of these emotions is one of the most healing aspects of any male/female relationship.

Men and Women in Trauma

Why tell you all of this? Quite simply, I don't want you to become reactive to one another in the middle of what you are experiencing. You are not going to change the differences between men and women. It is possible to accept them, appreciate them and understand them. To the extent that you can, you will be able to ease one another's burden brought on by the tragedy. If so, it is possible to give each other exactly what each needs.

The simple fact of the matter is that men and women are going to respond to crisis differently. Expecting each other to respond the way we "think they should" is to set ourselves up for failure. It's just not going to happen. You need to let that be okay.

It can be frustrating certainly, especially during a time like this when you feel like you don't have much left to give – especially to each other. You need each other in this time, and that need can become so overwhelming that it actually works against you. I want you to take a deep breath, be aware of what is really going on inside you and look deep within yourself to recognize what the other may need from you at this point in time. Identify what you expect from your spouse or partner. Is it realistic? Are you angry with him because he doesn't cry like you think he should with the reality of what has happened? Are you angry with her because she is always wanting to "talk about it"?

Understand that a woman's need to process all of this is going to be ultra-heightened. If there was ever a time when she needs to process, it is now – and that processing may take place often. She may feel the need to revisit conversations you have had already. Remember... she is trying to connect the dots.

A man may be tempted to inquire, "Haven't we already talked about this?" Resist the temptation! You know it's coming... understand that the need for a woman to talk about it again – and again – is part of her need to connect.

When the unthinkable happens, all of reality has been altered. Hence, it is going to take some time for equilibrium to be re-established. Rushing that process will frustrate a woman immensely – and the man who is hoping to be her helpmate through all of this. Women don't want to be rushed. It is why a woman can talk on the phone with her sister or friend for hours on end. They take their time, they re-visit stories often and they want to fully exhaust all the possible words that can be said about something. In the end, their stress is relieved and reconnection occurs.

Conclusions

So... conclusions. Men... listen and validate. It's the best thing you can do. It works to your benefit... the more you do this, the more she will be willing to give you the freedom to go to your "nothing" room.

When the female in your life needs to express herself, she is not asking for you to solve, fix, answer or decide anything. If she were, she would let you know. In this time, she needs you to understand the depth of her need to make sense of what happened – after all, it affected EVERYTHING in her room. Everything. As such, her world is in a state of chaos. She will bring equilibrium to it herself by using you as a partner in processing. Trust me... eventually she will settle in a place of contentment if you chose to actively participate with her in this process.

Women... let him go play golf or hunt or go to his nothing room. Tell him what you need – be specific and don't expect him to guess. After all, he can't read your mind. If you need/want him for something, tell him.

Do not misunderstand if he struggles with sitting in the hospital room or staying at home – he cannot fix anything there and it makes it worse for him. Give him specific things to do – pick up the kids, drop this off, or call so-and-so. It gives him something to do.

Read each other's waves... by doing so, you are setting yourself up for success – something you could use during your times of trial.

CHAPTER EIGHT

Finding Your Way Through The Grief Of Death

This is the hardest chapter to write – and read. If you have been through tragedy that has resulted in the death of a loved one, I can only imagine the depth of pain you are in right now. My heart goes out to you.

I wish there was something I could say to ease your pain.

But I know there isn't.

There are no words to express what you have been going through and what has been your experience. Honestly, not much – if anything – is more painful.

I have spent countless hours with parents, couples, and families who have lost precious loved ones – including their children. There is no easy answer that makes everything okay again. There just isn't – and you know that. So, let me do my best to walk with you for a brief moment in this chapter so as to give you some thoughts on grief and to help normalize that which you might be feeling.

Grief

Right up front, I want you to know that there is no way *around* this.

The only way is *through* it.

I want to give you permission to grieve. Not that you need it, but often I find that the people around us want the grieving to end so *they* can once again feel comfortable around us. You may have felt that, and I want you to know – that's about them, not you. The truth is, the closer the person was to you who has passed away, the deeper the depth of grief. And, that will take time. Lots of time. And you know what? You can take all the time you need.

Healing doesn't begin without grieving. Avoiding it, running from it, or denying it doesn't make the pain go away. Those methods have been tried and have been found wanting. You cannot heal without expressing your grief outwardly.

This is important to own... **Grief is a process, not an event.** The process is like a roller coaster. You may feel fine for a few days and – all of a sudden out of nowhere – you go downhill. I want you to understand that this is all normal. The pain you feel will not last forever if you choose to embrace it.

On occasion, I hear people say that, if they embrace their grief, it makes it real. The problem is... it is real! We cannot change what has happened, we can only move toward acceptance of what has happened. As hard as that is – as painful as that is – the journey toward healing demands it. Fighting acceptance only makes the pain and hurt last even longer.

That's something that people have a hard time grasping at the beginning of their journey through grief. The overwhelming pain that never seems to go away in the beginning does lessen over time. While the feeling of loss never completely goes away, thinking that you have to "get over it" only sets you up to fail in your grief.

Grief does not necessarily get easier day by day. Some days will be harder than the previous day. But, the pain will lessen over time. Taking life one day at a time becomes a motto to live by. Remember, with the hurt comes the healing.

One of the things that is detrimental is to say "I'm doing well" when it is obvious you are not. When we send the message that "we're okay therefore you can be okay" we are sending a message that sets us up for failure. However, I realize that it is impossible to be honest with certain people about what is really going on in you. In those cases, protecting yourself from more pain is completely understandable.

Generally, people know you are in pain. What they hope for is that your pain doesn't make them feel uncomfortable. Hence, they are relieved when they hear from you, "I'm doing well." If you are, fine. But if you're not...

Being honest is sometimes painful – you may not know how the other person is going to react – but you must remain true to yourself, who you are, and the depth of love you had for the one who has passed away. In essence, you honor them by being honest about how you feel.

Showing strong emotions can get you labeled "over-emotional" by some, but their labeling is typically the result of never having experienced a loss like yours. They have no right to say a word. You have EVERY right to mourn and grieve.

Truthfully, expressing emotions is central to life. Allow yourself to cry, be angry, feel deeply. This is healthy. Emotions are also a pathway to healing. If you have received the shame-based message that emotions are a sign of weakness, pay no attention to it (and consider the source). Your emotions will help you heal. They will move you toward your pain which is also the same direction as your healing.

Grief Over Time

Your relationship to your loved one who has passed away is unique. Because of this your grief process will be unique, too. Don't expect your grief to be similar to what you have seen in others. There are several factors which can affect your grief process:

- "Survival guilt" – You may feel like it "should have been me."
- You had to be the one to make the choice to take the loved one off life support.
- How your loved one passed away.
- The age of your loved one.
- Whether you had the opportunity to say "goodbye."
- Whether you were there when the trauma took place.

- You feel like you are the reason that your loved one passed away.

Whatever the case, you need to have places – safe places – where you can process the grief you are experiencing. Above all else, you need to talk about your loss. Those who would tell you that you "need to be over it by now" are not the ones with whom you should be talking. There is no time-table on your grief. "Getting over it" is not the point. How can you get over the loss of a child or spouse? It is about growing through it. It is about finding peace, meaning and acceptance. That takes time. And, in some cases... lots of time.

Having safe places to grieve – days, weeks, months, even years after the loss – is vital to your process. Being able to talk – and talk some more – means everything. You may not want to, you may not feel like it, and you may feel like you "should be past it" yourself. But, I am here to tell you that grief comes at various times and in various ways and having safe places to talk is THE biggest thing you can have.

You may have heard about the "stages of grief" and may think there is a sequential order you must go through. That is not necessarily the case. More than likely, you will experience stages in sporadic order and probably more than once. The key is to move through the process so that you can get to the place of acceptance – when you are ready. Remember... when YOU are ready and in YOUR time. There is no time table for "stages", there is no agenda on how fast or slow you are supposed to do this, and there is no "right way" to grieve. The point is to grieve... in your way and in your time.

Don't be surprised to experience pain on certain birthdays, holidays, or the anniversary of your loved one's death. Your body will know it. Those days will be hard. Knowing this, don't fall victim to them by trying to avoid those days altogether. It won't work. Instead, have a plan. *Be intentional.*

How do you want to make it through that day? You may want to visit the grave site, plant a tree, do something for someone else, volunteer at your favorite charity, release some balloons, or throw a party in your loved one's honor. Think about what you need and communicate it to those around you. Do not be afraid to ask for what you need.

The worst thing to do is stay in bed, shut the blinds and isolate yourself from the world. You are guaranteeing depression by doing that. You deserve better – the memory of your loved one deserves better – and you have the power and strength to make it happen.

One Last Thing

The concept of grief applies to everyone, even those who haven't lost a loved one. It is important to understand, accept and embrace. But please remember this: Grief is yours. You own it. You proceed through it. And you are better for having embraced it.

It may not feel like that right now.

It doesn't have to stay like this. And there are better days ahead, if you choose...

CHAPTER NINE

Finding Your Way To A New "New Normal"

Before tragedy struck, your life was "normal." But since it happened, life has been anything but "normal." While the shock of this has been nothing short of earth-shattering for you and yours, I want you to know this: you have all the power to create a "new normal" for yourself and your family. You do. The choices you make, the attitudes you take on and the way you find meaning in all of this will ultimately lead to your "new normal." And truth be told, that new normal does not have to be worse than what you formerly knew. In fact, it could be even better.

Do you remember where we started? It was with the whole image of a tsunami – huge crashing waves that pound your shore in search of their next phase of destruction. Waves so big that the very thought of them evokes fear in the pit of your stomach, throwing you into an abyss of anxiety and confusion.

But... the tsunami is not the end of the story. The waters that run in this ocean of life are not just destructive. Truly, most waves are meant to be enjoyed. It's why one of the first things a surfer learns is how to read the waves in order to get the best ride. That's what I hope you have gained through reading this. I hope you can see waves more clearly now for what they are – the ones to avoid and the ones to fully engage so that they might take you on a great ride.

I trust I have given you a lot of encouragement in these pages. First and foremost, I have stated that you can make it through this. And you will, if you so choose. Secondly, I have stated that you have what it takes to make it through this. And you do, since the choice is yours. Thirdly, I have said that there is a better story ahead for you and your family. I know this because I have lived it.

And there is for you – if you choose.

You can do this!

But there's one last thing. And it's big. It is the one thing that lights the way on your journey to recovery and joy.

Hope.

I used to think that hope was a cruel thing. You hope and hope and hope, only to be let down in the end. I used to think that hope plays you for a sucker, teasing that life can one day be good again, cards can fall into place and the stars can align the right way. I used to think that hope set up false expectations that could not possibly be realized. I used to believe that hope played on the vulnerability of humans too small and too naïve to face reality.

136

Like I said... I used to believe that.

I no longer do.

There are many, many wonderful things in this life. However, for the family who has experienced the family trauma tsunami, hope just may be the best of them all. Not too long ago, I started to think about all of the challenges I have faced thus far in my life. I then started to think about how often hope played a role in helping me with those challenges and obstacles.

Hope helped me walk again.

Hope brought my sister home from the hospital.

Hope let me play volleyball again.

Hope brought my family to new places of love and grace.

Hope led me to pursue a counseling degree and graduate level studies.

Hope helped me believe that anything was possible.

Hope allowed me to once again experience "life to the fullest."

Hope led me from my own tsunami of trauma to a sandy beach filled with wonderful waves to enjoy and ride.

Hope is the perfect antidote to fear. It is the jolt of energy, the shot of belief, the adrenaline rush of conviction that pushes a person past doubt, anxiety, worry, and fear over what is to come. It digs deep, finding that something inside you that gives you the strength to take on the challenges that await. It never gives up, never compromises and never stays stuck in a message of shame that seeks to rust and destroy.

Hold onto hope. In those moments when you are at your wit's end... In those times when you don't feel you can take it anymore... In those pauses of suffering silence... In those minutes of severe doubt... In the seemingly infinite waves of desperation... hold onto hope.

The truth is, a better story awaits you if you choose to engage it. What you are in right now is not the final chapter. This is not the end. You have more to add to the story of your life and, make no mistake... YOU write the story of YOUR life.

I don't know what that story is – what it will be like and where it will take you – and neither do you, for that matter. But I can promise you that – if you choose -- you will emerge from this trauma you have experienced, and you will be better, your family will be better, and the life story you write will be better.

There will come a day when you will be thankful for parts of the trauma you have been through.

Don't hear me wrong. That's not to say that you will be "glad" all of this happened. This isn't some sort of silly verbage that sweeps the trauma away as if it were nothing. Not at all. What I said was, there will come a day when you will be *thankful* for parts of the trauma you have been through. You will be thankful for who you have become. You will be thankful for where your family has arrived. You will be thankful for what you have achieved. You will be thankful for the life you now possess. You will be thankful for the lives you have been able to change because of your story.

That type of gratitude is a humbling, yet deeply enriching thing. It is what gives life its meaning. My prayer is that one day you will find it.

My hope for you is that you will sit on an ocean beach one day recalling the many days of journey through your trauma tsunami and find yourself at peace. I hope the incoming surf will remind you of the good waves you chose to ride that helped your journey turn out well.

Sometimes, the waves just stop pounding.

I pray and hope that you will arrive there one day.

And you will, if you so choose. Wonderful crystal clear waters framed by beautiful sunlit beaches await.

The choice is yours.

And remember, you really can do this...

If you loved How Could This Happen please go to Amazon and Barnes & Noble and leave your review.

Kristi loves feedback you can reach her on her website kristifowler.net Facebook or Twitter or email her at kristi@find-my-way.com

About the Author

Kristi was born in Bellingham, Washington, and grew up in Lynden, WA, a small farming community located near the Canadian border. An outstanding student and athlete in high school, Kristi pursued her education at Northwest Nazarene College in Nampa, Idaho, where she was a nationally-ranked setter for the women's volleyball team before graduating magna cum laude in 1993.

With a BA in Compassionate Ministries, Kristi followed it up with a Master's degree in Marital and Family Therapy and a Master's degree in Theology from Fuller Theological Seminary. Kristi has been a licensed Marriage and Family Therapist since 2000 and has worked in the private sector and church contexts to provide affordable therapy and counseling for individuals and couples throughout her career. She served as the Pastor of Enrichment Ministries at 7,000 member Lake Avenue Church in Pasadena, California from and also as the

Pastor of Community Compassion at Pasadena First Church of the Nazarene.

Since moving to Twin Falls, Idaho, Kristi has worked in private practice, specializing in the areas of marital therapy, parenting, women's issues and trauma. In addition, she gives community resource support to kids and families at the local Boys & Girls Club and serves on the Board of the Idaho Association of Marriage and Family Therapists. Kristi's latest project has been developing educational and therapeutic strategies for parents and families of children with trauma – specifically as it relates to the other children in the home.

Kristi knows firsthand about this issue from her own experience, having grown up in a family in which a tragic fire severely burned her older sister. She continues to work with individuals who have life issues from similar experiences and seeks to create safe places for them to find redemptive healing. A dynamic speaker and presenter, Kristi brings out in people and groups the ability to see things in a new perspective through her honesty, humor and passionate stories .

An avid athlete, Kristi enjoys working out each day and finding time to enjoy a variety of outdoor activities. She also enjoys baking, spending time with her husband and family, and a couple of really good TV shows. She and her husband, Sam, have two children, Cody (12) and Kendra (10).

www.ingramcontent.com/pod-product-compliance
Lightning Source LLC
Chambersburg PA
CBHW060939040426
42445CB00011B/927